Human Rights
in
Soviet
Society

Human Rights in Soviet Society

Konstantin U. Chernenko

INTERNATIONAL PUBLISHERS, New York

119012

JC
599
.S58
C4813

Library of Congress Cataloging in Publication Data

Chernenko, Konstantin Ustinovich.
  Human rights in Soviet society.

  Translation of: SSSR—KPSS, sotsialisticheskoe
obshchestvo, prava cheloveka.
  English title of Russian ed.: USSR—The Communist
party, socialist society, human rights. Moscow, 1981.
  Includes bibliographical references.
  1. Civil rights—Soviet Union. I. Title.
JC599.S58C4813   323.4'0947   81-6948
ISBN 0-7178-0588-3 (pbk.)   AACR2

CONTENTS

Konstantin U. Chernenko

ABOUT THE AUTHOR

Konstantin Ustinovich Chernenko is a Member of the Political Bureau of the CPSU Central Committee and Secretary of the CPSU Central Committee.

Konstantin Chernenko was born on September 24, 1911, in Siberia, into the family of a poor peasant. He has been a member of the Communist Party of the Soviet Union since 1931. When he was young he worked as a farmhand for well-to-do peasants. Since 1929, he has held many posts in the Komsomol and Communist Party organizations.

From 1941–1943, he was Secretary of the Krasnoyarsk Territory Party Committee. After graduating from the CPSU Central Committee Higher Party Organizers School, he was elected Secretary of the Penza Regional Party Committee. In 1948 he was appointed Head of the Propaganda Department of the Central Committee of the Moldavian Communist Party.

From 1960–1965, he headed the Secretariat of the Presidium of the USSR Supreme Soviet. Since 1965, he has been a department head of the CPSU Central Committee and since 1976, Secretary of the CPSU Central Committee. From 1977–1978, he was an Alternate Member of the Political Bureau of the CPSU Central Committee. Since 1978, he has been a full Member of the Political Bureau of the CPSU Central Committee. He has been elected a Deputy to the Supreme Soviet of the USSR since 1966. He has twice been awarded the title of Hero of Socialist Labor.

Human Rights in Soviet Society

INTRODUCTION

The freedom of the individual and democracy, human rights, equality and humanism—these major issues of our day are at the center of the ideological struggle between the two systems, socialism and capitalism, between the new and old worlds. As the socialist community and the communist and working-class movement become stronger and more influential, and as the liberation struggle of the peoples broadens, Western propagandists try to present imperialism as a champion of democracy, humaneness and justice. They lay particular stress on the "innate" rights of man unconnected with any socioeconomic formation, resort to insinuations and falsify the state of affairs in the Soviet Union and other socialist countries.

The U.S.-organized campaign in "defense" of human rights, which are allegedly violated in the socialist countries, and especially in the Soviet Union, has assumed a political as well as an ideological character. The U.S. government had declared the "defense of human rights" was becoming a central plank of its foreign policy, and said that it would concentrate its fire on violations of human rights in the communist countries.

The debate foisted upon us provides a good opportunity for comparing the socialist and capitalist ways of life, the real rights and freedoms enjoyed by people in the Soviet Union and in the United States. "We have no reason to shun any serious discussion of human rights," Leonid Brezhnev said. "Our revolution and the victory of socialism in this country have not only proclaimed but have secured in reality the rights of the working man, whatever his nationality, the rights of millions of working people in a way capitalism has been unable to do in any country of the world."

The USSR Constitution adopted in 1977 proclaims a whole number of rights and freedoms encompassing all spheres of economic, political, social and cultural life. In Lenin's words, in our country the "chief stress is shifted *from* formal *recognition* of liberties (such as existed under bourgeois parlimentarism) *to* actually ensuring the *enjoyment* of liberties by the working people who are overthrowing the exploiters . . . "[1] The new Constitution of the USSR not only considerably extends the range of the rights and freedoms of Soviet people, but marks an important step in further strengthening their guarantees.

In the West, the concept of human rights is often limited to exclude social and economic rights. Thus, for example, the right to work, to free higher education or to free qualified medical service are not found in the majority of bourgeois constitutions. Aren't these criteria for assessing the social maturity of society and its progress? In the USSR the concept of human rights, in addition to political and personal rights, includes socioeconomic rights. In socialist democracy human rights are regarded as a single complex which defines the legal position of the individual. We in the Soviet Union are guided by the principle that it is socioeconomic rights and freedoms that constitute the real foundation for the enjoyment of political and personal rights.

A citizen can feel really free and equal only when he is free from exploitation and social oppression, when he is assured of the possibility of taking part in running state and social affairs. We believe that truly free man is one who feels confident of tomorrow, who knows that he will never be deprived of the means of subsistence and who is sure that the state stands guard over his rights and freedoms, and that his

[1] V.I. Lenin, *Collected Works,* Vol. 27, p. 155.

rights and freedoms rest on a firm material foundation. In the system of socialist economy, which rules out appropriation by any one person of the results of another's labor, and which provides all people with access to material and cultural values, this becomes a reality.

The fruitfulness of such an approach to human rights is confirmed once again by recent UN decisions. In a resolution adopted by the Third Committee (dealing with social, humanitarian and cultural matters), in December 1980, it is stated that to fully guarantee the human rights of man and the dignity of the individual it is necessary to guarantee the right to work, the participation of working people in government, as well as the right to education, medical assistance and adequate nutrition, and that equal attention should be paid to the protection of civil, political and economic, as well as social and cultural rights.

Not surprisingly, the United States voted against this resolution, which speaks of the necessity of guaranteeing those rights that are absent in the U.S.

The Soviet conception of human rights in no way contradicts the principles of the most important international documents, including the Universal Declaration of Human Rights adopted more than three decades ago, and more recent documents such as the International Covenant on Economic, Social and Cultural Rights and the International Covenant on Civil and Political Rights. In fact, Soviet legislation in this sphere goes much further than the international covenants, for it provides for broader guarantees of the rights and freedoms of the individual.

For instance, the International Covenant on Economic, Social and Cultural Rights envisages the right of every person to education. In the USSR, not only primary, but also secondary and higher education is free. Another article of the same covenant speaks of the right to health protection, including medical assistance and care in the event of illness. The USSR Constitution provides not only for free and qualified medical assistance to all citizens in the event of illness, but also for a whole number of other measures aimed at protecting the health of citizens and ensuring them a long and active life. The Soviet

Union was one of the first states in the world to include the right to housing in its Fundamental Law. This right is not to be found in the international human rights covenants.

The Communist Party of the USSR (CPSU) is the ruling party; it has played, and plays now, a special role in elaborating the human rights concept, in defining the character and the order of priorities of measures ensuring these rights, and in organizing the entire life of society on socialist principles, without private ownership of the means of production, without the struggle for existence which, in the West, is called competition and which, in our view, makes their proclaimed human rights a mere formality in many respects.

The CPSU was the inspirer and organizer of the drafting and adoption of all Soviet constitutions.

The 26th Congress of the CPSU stated that our principal aim is to achieve lasting world peace and the well-being of the people. The program for further improving the well-being of Soviet people and for consolidating the material and intellectual foundations of the socialist way of life provides conditions for the ever fuller development of the political, civil, socioeconomic and cultural rights and freedoms of the individual.

The path to comprehensive and guaranteed rights and freedoms in their present form in the Soviet Union has been long and difficult. There was no example and experience to draw upon, means were lacking and wars interfered. How we began, what difficulties and obstacles we surmounted and what we have finally achieved are what this book is about.

I. RIGHTS AND FREEDOMS

DEMOCRACY, EQUALITY AND

FREEDOM OF THE INDIVIDUAL

The USSR Constitution guarantees to Soviet people a broad complex of political rights and freedoms:

- The right to take part in the management and administration of state and public affairs and in the discussion and adoption of laws and decisions of all-Union and local significance;
- The right to submit proposals to state agencies and public organizations for improving their activity, and to criticize shortcomings in their work;
- Freedom of speech, of the press and of assembly, street processions and demonstrations; the right to associate in public organizations.

All these rights and freedoms have a clearly expressed aim: to draw the broad mass of the people into the management of the state and society. This is the essence of socialist democracy. Lenin said: "Political liberty means the freedom of the people to arrange their public, state affairs."[1]

[1]V.I. Lenin, *Collected Works,* Vol. 6, p. 366.

Communists are convinced that there is no such thing as "pure democracy" or political rights and freedoms in general. Our political system is a complex of state and public organizations which help the working people manage all the affairs of society.

The people are led by the Communist Party, which has proved capable of *"leading the whole people* to socialism, of directing and organizing the new system, of being the teacher, the guide, the leader of all the working and exploited people in organizing their social life without the bourgeoisie and against the bourgeoisie."[1]

Having come into being earlier than the state and public organizations, the Party can be said to have stood at their cradle; it fostered them, helping them to gain strength and become powerful factors in social life. Historical experience shows that Party leadership is the principal source of their strength, the decisive precondition of their successful activity. Nationwide recognition of the role and importance of the party is reflected in the constitutional provision which says: "The leading and guiding force of Soviet society and the nucleus of its political system, of all state organizations and public organizations, is the Communist Party of the Soviet Union. The CPSU exists for the people and serves the people."

Party leadership is first of all political leadership. The CPSU determines the general perspectives of the development of society and the course of the country's domestic and foreign policy. It serves as a compass for state and public organizations by helping them to steer a correct course, to avoid a narrow departmental approach, to plan their work so that it should further the interests of the whole people.

The work of the Party has nothing in common with coercion and bureaucratic administration; it rests entirely on persuasion, on ideological influence. State and public organizations independently decide matters that are within their jurisdiction. The Communist Party pursues its policy in them primarily through

[1]V.I. Lenin, *Collected Works,* Vol. 25, p. 409.

Communists holding elective posts or working in the apparatus of state and public agencies.

Party organizations in the USSR function within the framework of the Constitution. Party members enjoy no special privileges compared with non-Party people. The CPSU does not promulgate laws. This is done by the USSR Supreme Soviet, the highest body of state authority in the country. The Party gives no instructions to the courts; to do so would be an encroachment on the independence of the judges and people's assessors as affirmed by Article 155 of the Constitution.

Under mature, developed socialism, the further extension of socialist democracy is the main goal in the development of the political system of Soviet society. The Party works tirelessly to secure ever broader participation of the people in managing state and public affairs, in improving the machinery of state, in heightening the activity of public organization, in strengthening the legal foundations of state and public life, and in achieving greater openness and constant responsiveness to public opinion. ". . . Along with the development of socialist democracy," Leonid Brezhnev said, "our statehood is gradually being transformed into communist social self-government. This is, of course, a long process, but it is proceeding steadily."[1]

[1] L.I. Brezhnev, *Our Course: Peace and Socialism* . . . , 1978, p. 150.

ALL POWER TO THE SOVIETS

Citizens of the USSR have the right to take part in the management and administration of state and public affairs . . . From Article 48 of the USSR Constitution.

After the victory of the Great October Socialist Revolution the drawing of the working people into managing state and public affairs was an indispensable prerequisite for building a new society. Our Party regarded it as its most important task to help workers and peasants to realize that they alone were now the masters of the country, of all its riches. "Remember," Lenin said, "that now *you yourselves* are at the helm of the state. No one will help you if you yourselves do not unite and take into *your* hands *all affairs* of the state."[1] For the first time in the history of civilized societies, the mass of the population was to take part freely, not only in voting and elections but also in day-to-day management.

Of course, in the beginning the working people had no experience in running the state. This experience could not be gained by attending meetings, hearing lectures or reading pamphlets written by Communists. It could be acquired only through practice; and the first socialist transformations showed that rank-and-file workers could not only destroy the old system, but could also build life on new, socialist principles. The promotion of workers and peasants to leading posts in state and economic agencies made them aware that they were the masters of the country, that power now lay in their hands.

In its *Second Program* (1919) the Communist Party set the task of "gradually drawing the entire working population into the work of governing the state." It has invariably pursued this goal at all stages of socialist and communist construction.

[1] V.I. Lenin, *Collected Works,* Vol. 26, p. 297.

In the years of Soviet power the political consciousness and political activity of the working people have grown immeasurably. From among the working masses there have emerged millions of able organizers, government workers, economic executives, scientists and workers in the field of culture. A system of political institutions ensuring all people every opportunity to participate directly in managing state and public affairs has been set up and has stood the test of time.

Our country is sometimes simply called the Soviets.[1] *The Soviets of People's Deputies constitute the political foundation of our state. They are organs of representative democracy through which the people exercise their state power.*

The whole history of our socialist state is intrinsically linked with the Soviets. They came into being on the initiative of workers three quarters of a century ago, in the fire of the first Russian revolution, as organs of the working people's struggle against the autocracy, and in defense of the interests of the working people. Lenin immediately saw that the Soviets were the embryo of a revolutionary government, that they were new organs of people's power. Under the slogan "All Power to the Soviets," the Party roused the working class and the poorest sections of the peasantry to overthrowing the power of estate owners and capitalists and led them to victory in the October Socialist Revolution. This slogan became the basis of Lenin's plan for building the new state as a republic of Soviets "from top to bottom."[2]

For the first time in history, all state power went into the hands of mass organizations consisting of workers and peasants. This Leninist principle of giving all power to the Soviets was affirmed in the Constitution of the Russian Federation of 1918, in the constitutions of the other union republics and then in the USSR Constitutions of 1924 and 1936. Preserving the continuity of the principles of the previous Soviet constitutions, the Constitution of 1977 says, in part: "The people exercise state power through Soviets of People's Deputies. . . . All other state

[1] *Soviet* means "council".
[2] V.I. Lenin, *Collected Works*, Vol. 24, p. 23.

bodies are under the control of, and accountable to, the Soviets of People's Deputies."

From the very beginning it was important, both politically and practically, to determine the place and role of the ruling Communist Party in the state of the Soviets. This was done by Lenin, who said: ". . . all the work of the Party is carried on through the Soviets, which embrace the working masses, irrespective of occupation."[1]

The Party invariably stressed the need for correctly combining the functions of Party and government bodies for their day-to-day interaction. It was pointed out in the resolution of the 8th Congress of the Communist Party: "On no account should the functions of Party collectives be mixed with those of government bodies, the Soviets . . . The Party endeavors to *guide* the activities of the Soviets, but not to supplant the latter."

From the very first days following the victory of the October Revolution the Party sought to secure the fullest possible realization of the vast potential of the Soviet form of government, to enhance the role of the Soviets in the revolutionary socialist reconstruction of society, and in every way helped to elaborate the principles, forms and methods of their activities. It made sure that the Soviets worked as institutions combining legislative and executive functions. Lenin said that ". . . the parliamentarians themselves have to work, have to execute their own laws, have to test the results achieved in reality themselves, and to account directly to their constituents."[2]

Eradicating illiteracy, helping the mass of the people to overcome their distrust of everything connected with state power and trying to do away with numerous nationalist and patriarchal prejudices, the Party sought to adapt, as far as possible, the organization and character of the work of the Soviets to the capabilities of the deputies.

In conditions of mature socialism, while creatively implementing the Leninist principles of giving all power to the Soviets, the Party does its utmost to strengthen the bodies of state power, to

[1]*Ibid.*, Vol. 31, p. 49.
[2]V.I. Lenin, *Collected Works*, Vol. 25, p. 429.

enhance their role in the life of society, to promote their initiative and escalate their activity. These questions occupy a prominent place in the decisions of Party congresses; they have been repeatedly discussed in the Party Central Committee. In recent years, on the Party's initiative, important measures have been carried out to strengthen the legal and material basis of the Soviets, and laws have been passed concerning the work of all the links of the Soviet system.

In accordance with the USSR Constitution, there is a single system of bodies of state authority consisting of the Supreme Soviet of the USSR, the Supreme Soviets of union and autonomous republics, and the Soviets of People's Deputies of territories, regions, areas, cities, districts, settlements and villages. At present there are more than 51,000 Soviets forming a pyramid with the USSR Supreme Soviet at the top.

The Soviets direct all sectors of state, economic, social and cultural development directly or through agencies set up by them. Of course they differ in "rank," scope of activity, and internal organization. But each Soviet is a component of state power. It is not only empowered to decide all matters within its jurisdiction; it also acts as the conduit of decisions of country-wide importance.

The highest body of state authority of the USSR is the Supreme Soviet of the USSR. It considers and approves state plans for economic and social development and the state budget, improves the country's legislation, conducts active and fruitful domestic and foreign policy work, supervises the work of all state agencies accountable to it and forms the Council of Ministers of the USSR, the highest executive and administrative body of state authority.

The Supreme Soviets of the union and autonomous republics are empowered to deal with all matters within the jurisdiction of the republics, and the local Soviets deal with those within the jurisdiction of the territories, regions, cities, etc.

The USSR Constitution guarantees to Soviet people the right to vote and to be elected to Soviets of People's Deputies. This is one of the most important guarantees of their right to take part in managing state and public affairs.

The right of working people to vote and to be elected to bodies of state authority was proclaimed in the first Soviet Constitution. But it disenfranchised all those who lived on unearned income and used hired labor, as well as clergymen, former policemen, etc. Besides, the franchise was not quite equal: the representation quotas in the Soviets for workers and peasants were different. Only city and rural Soviets were elected by direct ballot. All other bodies of state power were formed at respective congresses of Soviets. Voting in all elections was open.

The limitations with regard to the franchise were necessary because of the historical situation in which the Soviet Republic found itself. The propertied classes, with the backing of foreign imperialists, were waging an open war against the people and defied Soviet laws. A strong influence was wielded in the countryside by the "kulaks," rich peasants who relied on hiring farmhands. In such conditions, the disfranchisement of the propertied classes was part of the struggle against them, while the preference quotas strengthened the leading role of the working class in the state.

However, Lenin emphasized that these limitations were temporary, and that after the exploiting classes were abolished and the cause of socialism was consolidated, the Soviet state would be able to introduce, and would introduce, universal suffrage without any restrictions.

This was done with the entry into force of the USSR Constitution of 1936. Then all Soviets were elected on the basis of universal, equal, and direct suffrage by secret ballot. This means that the right to vote is given to all citizens of the USSR who have reached the age of 18; that each voter has one vote; that deputies to all Soviets are elected directly; that any control over the voters expressing their will is not permitted.

Bodies of state authority in the USSR are formed on broad democratic principles. The right to nominate candidates belongs to Party, trade union, Young Communist League (Komsomol), cooperative and other public organizations, work collectives, and meetings of servicemen in their units. The USSR Constitution guarantees a free and candid discussion of the political and personal qualities of candidates, and the right to campaign for them at meetings, in the press, on TV and radio. All expenses involved in holding elections are met by the state.

The people take an active part in the preparation and holding of elections. In the 1980 elections to the Supreme Soviets of the union and autonomous republics and the local Soviets, 936,800 electoral commissions were formed in which 8.6 million representatives of public organizations and work collectives took part. Ballots were cast by 176.6 million voters (99.9 percent), or by practically the entire adult population of the country.

Western propaganda points to universal suffrage as one of the most important indications of the democratic character of bourgeois parliamentarism. It forgets to mention that it is only in recent years—and only under the pressure of the working people—that restrictions on grounds of property status, sex, education, etc., which had for centuries been used to prevent working people from taking part in elections, were abolished or eased in capitalist countries. However, as before, various means are used to prevent free expression of the will of the electorate —such as artificial division of electoral districts, manipulations with different electoral systems, the bribing of voters, the rigging of elections, etc.

As a result, people lose interest in elections and many do not vote. Only 52.3 percent of those eligible to vote went to the polls in the 1980 presidential election in the United States. It is the lowest figure for elections in the last 32 years. This mass absenteeism is not merely a sign of indifference toward the "political process," as Western sociologists contend. It is an expression of the growing distrust of a system which offers no free choice. It shows that for tens of millions of Americans civil rights have lost much of their meaning—the very same civil rights that have become, on Washington's initiative, the chief item of the ideological export of imperialism.

As socialist and communist construction advanced, the social base of the Soviet form of democratic government broadened. This is reflected in the names of the Soviets. At first called Soviets of Workers', Peasants' and Red Army Men's Deputies, with the completion of socialist construction they became Soviets of Working People's Deputies, and when the state of the dictatorship of the proletariat had developed into a socialist state of the whole people, they became Soviets of People's Deputies.

The composition of the Soviets is proof of real democratic government in our country. At present they have a total of 2.3 million deputies representing all social groups, all the nations and nationalities of the Soviet Union. They are working people, the "powerful collective intellect of Soviet power," as Leonid Brezhnev has called the deputies.

More than two-thirds of all deputies are industrial workers and collective farmers and about one-third, teachers, doctors, scientific and cultural workers, workers of Party and public organizations, economic executives, servicemen, students and representatives of other categories of working people. Women make up almost half of the deputies; every third deputy is under 30 years of age; 43 percent are members and candidate members of the CPSU. It should be stressed at this point that there are no professional parliamentarians in the USSR. The deputies perform their duties without leaving their job. They remain at work with those whose worries, aspirations and needs are well known to them.

The composition of the USSR Supreme Soviet makes it possible to express fully the common will of the Soviet people and at the same time to take into consideration the specific interests of different classes, social groups, nations and nationalities. Among the 1,500 deputies of its two chambers, more than half are workers and collective farmers. Also widely represented are members of the intelligentsia engaged in the national economy; science, literature and the arts; education and health protection; party functionaries and public activists; economic executives; students; servicemen and other sections of the population. Among the deputie of the highest body of state authority are Party and government leaders and workers of trade union, Komsomol and other public organizations. Women account for 33 percent of the deputies and persons under 30 years of age, 20 percent; more than two-thirds are Communists.

People of 61 nationalities within the Soviet Union are included among the deputies.

It may be noted, for purposes of comparison, that the 535 members of the U.S. Congress include 243 lawyers, 140 businessmen, 47 persons who work in the field of education, 30 former government employees, 25 farmers, 18 former journalists and 32 others. There is not a single industrial worker among them. Ninety-five percent of the congressmen are white. In the FRG Bundestag, only 30 out of the 518 deputies are working-class background.

In the Soviet Union we follow the Leninist principle of unity of legislative and executive power. Deputies not only discuss and adopt laws and make decisions at sessions of the Soviets, but also conduct day-to-day practical work of managing state and public affairs. They organize and supervise the implementation of laws and decisions, check on the work of enterprises, organizations and institutions, consider constituents' complaints and requests, see to it that the voters' mandates are fulfilled, and so on. In the past decade the Soviets received 3,250 such mandates and carried out 2,950 of them. During sessions of Soviets, deputies widely exercise the right of asking questions as a means of controlling the work of executive bodies and office holders.

Specialized standing commissions of the Soviets are an important instrument of ensuring the effective participation of deputies in the work of bodies of power. At present there are more than 330,000 such commissions uniting more than 1.8 million deputies. Their functions include preliminary consideration and preparation of questions to be placed before sessions of the executive committees of the Soviets, control over the implementation of decisions adopted, etc.

Formation of deputy groups as a means of pooling the efforts of deputies on the scale of electoral districts is widely practiced.

The Law on the Status of Deputies clearly defines the rights and duties of deputies and the obligations of state and public organizations toward them. The powers of deputies are fixed in the Constitution.

All activities of the Soviets are conducted on a truly democratic basis, openly and under the control of the masses. The Soviets inform the population about the decisions adopted by them and about the results of their implementation. It has become traditional for executive committees and individual deputies to report to the electorate at regular meetings. For example, in 1979, deputies of local Soviets delivered reports at 3,767,000 meetings attended by a total of 198 million constituents. Of great importance is the constituents' right to recall deputies who have not justified their confidence.

The results of every election make significant changes in the composition of the Soviets. In the 1980 elections to the Supreme Soviets of the union and autonomous republics and local Soviets, 47 percent of the deputies were elected for the first time. Thus millions of Soviet people receive practical schooling in managing the state.

People's control agencies are an important element of Soviet democracy ensuring the citizens' right to take part in running state and public affairs.

From the simplest functions, like supervising the distribution of foodstuffs and the work of canteens, which, as Lenin wrote, was fully within the ability of every honest, intelligent and efficient worker and peasant,[1] to the analysis of highly complicated problems of economic and cultural development and managerial questions—such is the scope of work carried out by People's Control inspectors in our country.

People's Control committees, now truly on a mass scale, embracing practically every aspect of life, have become an organic part of the Soviet political system. They are formed by the Soviets and combine state control with public control. The basis of the system is made up of People's Control groups and posts (1.3 million in all) at industrial enterprises, on construction sites, on collective and state farms, in institutions, educational establishments, army units, ministries and departments. Members of the groups and posts (9.7 million people) are elected at meetings of work collectives and are accountable to them. Millions of activists from among workers, farmers and office employees take part in inspections organized by these groups

[1]V.I. Lenin, *Collected Works*, Vol. 26, p. 412.

and posts. The work of People's Control inspectors is given wide publicity. Their rights are protected by the Law on People's Control in the USSR.

The main tasks of People's Control committees are to help carry out Party and government decisions, plan assignments and combat violations of state discipline, mismanagement, red tape and bureaucracy. "Not a single violation, not a single case of abuse, wastage or lack of discipline," Leonid Brezhnev said at the 26th CPSU Congress, "should be overlooked by the People's Control inspectors. The CPSU Central Committee guides them toward more energetic and resolute action."

The Soviet Constitution ensures the right of citizens to run state and public affairs by enabling them to vote and to be elected to state bodies, to take part in their work. These bodies include, for instance, the courts.

On November 22, 1917, Lenin signed the Decree on the Courts, which established the principles of the Soviet judicial system: elected judges and people's assessors, public hearing of cases, guarantee of the right to defense and the participation of citizens in administering justice. These basic principles have stood the test of time and are enshrined in the USSR Constitution.

In the USSR there are the Supreme Court of the USSR; the Supreme Courts of the union and autonomous republics, territorial, regional; city, area and district courts and military tribunals in the armed forces. People's judges of district courts are elected by citizens by secret ballot, while people's assessors are elected at meetings of citizens at their places of work or residence by a show of hands. The judges of higher courts are elected by the corresponding Soviets. The judges and people's assessors are responsible and accountable to their electors or the bodies that have elected them and may be recalled by them in the manner prescribed by law.

In accordance with the USSR Constitution, the right of citizens to take part in government applies to the sphere of state as well as public activities. They can take part in the work of public organizations and voluntary public bodies and in meetings at places of work or residence.

An important place in Soviet society is occupied by work

collectives, which are the primary units not only of the economic, but also of the sociopolitical organism. Many important questions of state and public life, organization of production management, construction of houses and cultural facilities, etc. are discussed and decided at meetings of work collectives. The rights and duties of work collectives are defined in the Constitution.

The years of socialist and communist construction have witnessed a constant extension of the direct participation of millions of citizens in running state and public affairs. *Today it is a constitutional right of Soviet citizens to take part in the discussion and adoption of laws and decisions of all-Union and local importance and in nationwide referendums.*

It has become a tradition for all sections of the population to participate directly in discussing and deciding all major questions of the country's political, socioeconomic and cultural life. The drafts of decisions and laws bearing on the fundamental problems of the country's development are submitted for countrywide discussion. The drafts are published in the press, and everyone has the right and means to voice his or her opinion.

A good example is the nationwide discussion of the draft of the 1977 Constitution, in which more than 140 million people, or four-fifths of the country's adult population, took part. It is also significant that in recent years not a single state plan for the Soviet Union's economic development has been adopted without being thoroughly discussed not only by the Supreme Soviet, but also in work collectives and through the mass media. There were extensive discussions of the drafts of such important legislative acts as the fundamentals of legislation on labor, on marriage and the family, on housing construction, on pensions, on environmental protection and others.

Of course, direct expression of the will of the masses is not limited to nationwide discussions. For instance, the new Constitution gives citizens *the right to submit proposals to state bodies and public organizations for improving their activity, and to criticize shortcomings in their work.*

The Constitution makes it a duty of officals to examine citizens' proposals and requests within established time limits, to reply to them and to take appropriate action. Persecution for criticism is prohibited. Persons guilty of such persecution are called to account.

Soviet people widely use their constitutional freedom of speech, of the press, and of assembly, street processions and demonstrations. For this the state places at their disposal public buildings (club houses, palaces of culture, etc.), streets and squares, as well as the information media.

We highly value such forms of free expression of opinion as citizens' letters and oral addresses to state, Party and other bodies. They are an extremely important source of firsthand information, and we constantly emphasize the need for an attentive, responsive attitude to the opinions of the people. "It is the duty of every Party functionary, of every leader to the people and the Party to examine letters, requests and complaints from citizens with tact and consideration," Leonid Brezhnev said at the 26th CPSU Congress. Working with letters and oral statements is considered highly responsible work. One can speak here of an important political tradition in the establishment of which a notable part was played by Lenin. Letters addressed to him from working people and his talks with envoys sent by peasants gave him valuable information about the most pressing problems, which he summarized and took into consideration in political decisions.

The importance of this work is evidenced by the number of citizens' letters and requests. For instance, in the past five years (between the 25th and 26th Party congresses), the CPSU Central Committee received more than 3.2 million letters and oral requests. Fifteen million letters and oral requests were examined by local party committees.

The work of examining letters and analyzing and summarizing opinions, proposals and comments is part of the process of carrying out current and long-term tasks. Many such proposals are used when drafting important Party and government decisions and in the practical activities of leading Party and government bodies.

Ever broader and more active participation of the people in

managing state and public affairs has become the central trend of the political development of Soviet society. Leonid Brezhnev said: "Our Party has displayed, and will continue to display, constant concern to ensure that the working people don't merely possess the opportunities afforded by the Constitution for taking part in the administration of society, but are actually able to take part in it."

ORGANIZATIONS OF WORKING PEOPLE

> . . . Citizens of the USSR have the right to associate in public organizations . . . From Article 51 of the USSR Constitution

Whereas the Soviets, being a form of state authority, express primarily the interests of the whole people, the trade unions, the All-Union Leninist Young Communist League (Komsomol), the cooperatives, and sports, professional, defense and other societies and organizations express the specific interests and requirements of different social, professional, age and other groups.

Public organizations, which are set up on a strictly voluntary basis, work out and adopt their rules themselves and decide matters within their competence. All their activities rest on the basis of self-administration and other democratic norms and principles. Soviet legislation provides public organizations with conditions for their effective function, such as premises, transport, printing facilities, printing paper, information, media, etc.

In keeping with the USSR Constitution, the trade unions, the Komsomol, the cooperative and other public organizations participate, in accordance with the tasks defined in their rules, in managing state affairs and in deciding political, economic and sociocultural questions; they have the right to initiate legislation through their all-union bodies. Besides, some functions formerly performed by state agencies have been delegated to them.

Public organizations carry out their work in close interaction with the state. They are represented on the boards of ministries and departments. State agencies coordinate drafts of their decisions with public organizations, and they often adopt joint decisions.

Each public organization plays a special role in the political system of Soviet society, each has its own specific tasks and its own organizational structure. But at the same time each of them makes its contribution to the common cause of communist construction, the supreme goal which serves as the determining constitutional principle of their establishment and functioning.

An important place in the political system of socialism is occupied by trade unions. The biggest mass organizations of working people, they unite more than 129 million workers, farmers, office employees, and students of higher, specialized secondary and vocational training schools.

It was noted at the 26th Congress of the CPSU that the Party regards the trade unions as its reliable base of popular support, as a powerful means of promoting democracy and drawing people into the building of communism.

The trade unions are organized on the industrial principle. The employees of one enterprise or organization are members of one union. Wage-earning and salaried workers of enterprises and institutions belonging to one or several branches of the national economy are united in sectoral unions.

Every sectoral union is made up of primary organizations established at industrial enterprises, construction projects, on collective and state farms, at institutions, etc. Primary organizations are headed by factory and office committees elected at trade union meetings or conferences. Trade union committees are elected to give guidance to primary organizations of a particular branch of the economy on the scale of a district, city, territory or union republic, a railway line or a water basin. Each sectoral trade union has its Central Committee.

In the union republics, territories and regions, the activities of sectoral unions are coordinated and inter-union questions are decided by Councils of Trade Unions, and on the scale of the whole country, by the All-Union Central Council of Trade Unions (AUCCTU).

In Russia, trade unions first emerged at the height of the first Russian revolution (1905–1907), under the direct leadership of the Communist Party. Communists helped set up the unions, which they joined in order to work in them and resist attempts to limit the scope of the trade union movement and subordinate it to the entrepreneurs' interests.

The struggle for economic reforms, Communists said, was important but it could only improve the terms for the sale of labor power. To remove the reasons that compelled people to sell their labor power, revolutionary struggle for socialism was needed.

Under the guidance of the Communist Party, the trade unions headed the economic struggle of the proletariat of Russia against the capitalists; they did a great deal to organize the working people and to raise their class consciousness, and took an active part in the organization and accomplishment of the Great October Socialist Revolution.

Following the Revolution a virtually new type of trade union began to take shape in our country. In the first place, the economic basis of the exploitation of working people had been eliminated with the abolition of private ownership of the means of production, and with the working class becoming the master of factories and mills. A consequence of this, as Lenin noted, was that the trade unions no longer had "to face the *class* economic struggle."[1]

State power had passed into the hands of the working class. As a result, the trade unions became, in Lenin's words, the closest and most indispensable collaborator with the government.

Thus, the trade unions, formerly a weapon of struggle against

[1]V.I. Lenin, *Collected Works*, Vol. 32, p. 100.

the capitalists and the bourgeois state, became a constructive force in the building of socialism and communism.

Lenin thoroughly substantiated the role and place of the trade unions in the political system of Soviet society. The trade union, he pointed out, is "an organization designed to draw in and to train; it is, in fact, a school: a school of administration, a school of economic management, a school of communism."[1] "Being a school of communism in general," he stressed, "the trade unions must, in particular, be a school for training the whole mass of workers, and eventually all working people, in the art of managing socialist industry."[2] Lenin's ideas became the basis of the activities of Soviet trade unions.

Immediately following the October Revolution, before the state apparatus for managing the national economy was set up, the trade unions, alongside Workers' Control committees, were almost the only bodies which could and must undertake the work of organizing production and the management of enterprises. The First All-Russian Congress of Trade Unions, held in January 1918, said in its resolution: "The focus of the work of the trade unions must now be shifted to the organizational-economic sphere. Because they are the class organizations of the proletariat, set up on the industrial principle, the trade unions must undertake the principal work of organizing production and restoring the undermined productive forces of the country." Subsequently the trade unions conducted this work together with state bodies, whose weakness at this early stage justified such parallelism.

As the managerial apparatus became more efficient the Party pursued a policy of clearly demarcating the rights and duties of the trade unions from those of the economic bodies, and resolutely combatted attempts of some trade union officials to interfere directly and incompetently in the management of enterprises. It should be noted that in the first years of Soviet power the influence of petty bourgeois disorder was very

[1] Ibid., Vol. 32, p. 20.
[2] V.I. Lenin, *Collected Works*, Vol. 33, p. 190.

pronounced in our country, which inevitably caused many workers to veer toward anarchism. In particular, this found expression in the demands of the "workers' opposition" which amounted to handing over management of the national economy to "an All-Russia Congress of Producers organized in trade and industrial unions."[1] Objectively these demands were aimed at undermining the leading role of the Communist Party in building socialism, at downgrading and even putting a stop to the economic-organizational activity of the Soviet state.

Understandably, the demands of the "workers' opposition" were rejected, as was the stand of the Trotskyites who sought to turn the trade unions into a mere appendage of the state machinery.

The Party pointed out that the trade unions should "vigorously support the economic executives' measures aimed at raising labor productivity, harmoniously combining them with the interests of the workers whom they represent and with the possibility of maximally successful *implementation of these measures.*" At the same time the Party came out against the trade unions indiscriminately approving all the measures and proposals of the administration, forgetting that their principal function was to represent and defend the economic interests of the workers.

At all the stages of socialist and communist construction the Party has helped the trade unions to orient their activity toward effective defense of the workers' rights, constantly working for their vital interests. The trade unions have extensive possibilities —both legal and material—for this. In keeping with the country's law, not a single measure bearing on the interests of workers, collective farmers and salary earners, the conditions and remuneration for labor, social security, improvement of housing conditions and communal services and the raising of the standard of living is drafted and implemented without the participation of the trade unions.

All draft plans for individual branches of the economy and for the economy as a whole are considered by leading trade union

[1] V.I. Lenin, *Collected Works*, Vol. 32, p. 198.

bodies. Jointly with the USSR State Committee for Labor and Social Questions, the AUCCTU elaborates and approves the basic provisions on paying bonuses and documents determining rate setting. The wage scales and salaries of workers, engineers and technicians and managerial employees in all branches of the national economy are jointly approved by the AUCCTU and the government. On the trade unions' initiatives many important laws have been passed and decisions taken by the Party and the government aimed at improving working conditions, everyday life and rest and recreation of working people.

Extensive rights in deciding questions of economic activity are enjoyed by primary trade union organizations. These rights are enumerated in a special statute having the force of law. The committees of the primary trade union organizations take part in the drafting of plans for the socioeconomic development of work collectives and of plans for capital and housing construction and the provision of cultural and everyday amenities. They have the right to hear reports by economic executives on plan fulfillment, the results of production and economic activities, the implementation of measures for improving the organization and conditions of labor and providing cultural and other services to factory and office workers.

An important part of the work of trade union organizations is the conclusion of annual collective agreements between the management and the work collectives. These agreements envisage mutual responsibility in all matters involving worker-manager and leader-executor relations. They cover every aspect of the activity of the given enterprise or organization—from the introduction of new technology to the construction of a stadium, from technical retooling to the quality of dental service at the factory polyclinic. In signing such agreements the trade union committees, jointly with management determine how best to use the funds allocated for the development of the enterprises, for social and cultural undertakings, for housing construction and the granting of material incentives. Should disagreement arise between the administration and the trade union, the draft of the collective agreement is reviewed by higher trade union and economic bodies.

The trade unions see to it that both the work collectives and the management honor their commitments. An economic executive violating the provisions of the collective agreement is held strictly accountable.

The trade unions have the right to check on the observance of labor legislation and the organization of labor protection. An important part is played here by 6,200 trade union technical inspectors, who are accountable to the industrial and territorial trade union committees. Their instructions are binding for executives at all levels. A technical inspector has the right to go to any enterprise and check on the conditions there; he can impose a fine on a foreman or a director-general and raise the question of closing a shop or even a whole enterprise where safety-engineering and labor protection rules are violated.

Without the consent of the trade union committee the management cannot dismiss an employee or put into operation any new production facilities. Work quotas introduced without previous consultation with the trade union organization are invalid.

In 1979, 6,174 executives were called to administrative account and 146 dismissed from their posts at the demand of trade unions for failing to provide adequate labor protection, prevent industrial accidents and carry out other obligations under collective agreements.

Defense of the rights and interests of the working people has always been and will be the most important function of trade unions. Naturally, in a socialist country the political and socioeconomic basis of this "protecting function" is not the same as in the West. In the former, the factory manager striving to increase the profits of the enterprise and the trade union committee striving to raise the standard of living of the personnel serve equally the interests of the working people. And the trade unions, in concerning themselves with the interests of industrial and office workers, cannot help but concern themselves with the development of the national economy, with increasing production and improving its quality indicators. Such, Leonid Brezhnev said, is the "dual task" of the trade unions.

The trade unions effectively influence the operation of enterprises through the standing production committees, elected at workers' meetings. At present there are more than 139,000 such committees in the country. They unite a total of 6 million people, two-thirds of whom are workers. The rights and duties of the production committees are determined by a special statute approved by the USSR Council of Ministers and the AUCCTU. In keeping with the statute, the committees consider questions of planning and introduction of new technology, adopt decisions and submit proposals whose implementation is organized by economic executives. In the last two years these proposals affected areas of the economy worth 1.4 billion rubles.[1] By taking part in production conferences the workers master the skills of running enterprises.

The trade unions also direct the work of the All-Union Society of Inventors and Innovators, scientific and technical societies, and innovators' councils, whose members are creative-minded workers and engineers.

In the USSR trade unions manage the state social insurance system directly. They run 930 sanatoria, holiday hotels and holiday homes, almost 2,500 after-work sanatoria, nearly 1,000 tourist centers, hotels and campgrounds, and more than 57,000 Young Pioneer summer camps. At their disposal are 22,200 clubhouses, houses and palaces of culture, over 56,000 film-projection units and more than 19,000 libraries. They also direct the work of 33 sports societies, which have a total of 2,800 stadiums, 12,300 gymnasiums, almost 900 swimming pools, 5,300 skiing centers, and 4,800 sports and health-building camps. The trade unions also have their own publishing houses which put out newspapers, magazines and books.

The trade unions have big tasks and enjoy exceedingly broad rights. But as noted at the 26th Congress of the CPSU, sometimes they lack initiative in exercising these rights. The congress called for greater control by the trade unions and work collectives over decisions affecting the work and lives of people and their broader participation in planning and managing production, selecting and placing personnel and effectively using the funds at the disposal of enterprises and organizations.

[1]One ruble equals $1.60.

Many leading posts in the trade unions are held by Communists. As the 11th Party Congress (1922) stressed in its decisions, Communists promoted to trade union posts "should live the life of workers, know it thoroughly, be able to assess correctly the frame of mind of the masses on any question, their true aspirations, requirements and thoughts, to ascertain without a shade of false idealization the degree of their political consciousness and the strength of the influence of some of other prejudices and traces of the past, and be able to win the boundless trust of the masses by taking a comradely attitude to them, by working hard for the satisfaction of their requirements." These demands remain valid today.

The mass youth organization, Komsomol, plays an active role in the sociopolitical life of the country. The Komsomol has a membership of more than 40.5 million young men and women —young workers and farmers, office employees, students and young members of the military. A total of 23.6 million Komsomol members work in various branches of the national economy.

The Komosomol is organized on the territorial production principle: Primary organizations set up at places of work or study unite to form district, city and area organizations, which, in turn, form the Komsomol organizations of regions, territories and union republics. The highest body of the Komsomol is its congress, and in the interim between congresses—the Central Committee of the Komsomol.

The history of the Komsomol is inseparably linked with the name of Lenin and the activities of the Communist Party. The first revolutionary youth organizations were formed after the bourgeois-democratic revolution of February 1917. At that time the 6th Congress of the Party, attaching great importance to this movement, adopted a special resolution which said, in part: "Our Party should . . . strive to ensure that working youth establish autonomous organizations that are not subordinated organizationally to the Party and are only linked with it ideologically. At the same time, the Party wants these organizations to assume a socialist character from the outset . . . *Intervention by the Party in the organization of the working youth should not be in the nature of tutelage over it.*"

The socialist leagues of young workers and peasants became the Party's militant helpers, one of the strike detachments of the revolutionary proletariat in the days of the Great October Socialist Revolution.

The 1st All-Russia Congress of Working and Peasant Youth Leagues (October 1918), convened on Lenin's initiative, proclaimed the establishment of the Komsomol—the Russian Young Communist League. For the first time in the history of the revolutionary movement, a youth organization of a new type was created—proletarian in nature, communist in aims and tasks and mass-oriented and autonomous in character.

In the resolution "On Work Among Youth", adopted by the 8th Party Congress, it was said: "Communist work among young people can proceed successfully only through autonomous youth organizations marching under the banner of communism, where young people could display maximum independence, which is indispensable to their communist education. The Russian Young Communist League is such an organization . . . The 8th Congress of the Russian Communist Party regards the continued existence and further development of the Russian Young Communist League as necessary. The Russian Communist Party should give the most active ideological and material support to the Russian Young Communist League."

The role and place of the Komsomol in the life of the country and the program for youth education were determined in Lenin's speech "The Tasks of the Youth Leagues," delivered at the 3rd Congress of the Russian Young Communist League in 1920. This speech is the most important theoretical document of our Party on the communist education of young people.

The Party pointed out that the Russian Young Communist League, through which the Party exerted its influence on the broad masses of young people and which had specific tasks that differed from those of the Party, should be a self-governing organization. At the same time it combatted tendencies to place the youth organization at a distance from the Party, which could be observed among a certain section of the Komsomol membership (theories of "neutrality", "equality", etc.), and stressed that without leadership by the Party the Komsomol would be unable to perform its tremendous role in the sociopolitical life of the country. The Party taught the Russian Young Communist League to link the personal and group interests of young men and women with the interests of the working class, to subordinate day-to-day work to the common revolutionary tasks of the proletariat.

The Komsomol was named after great Lenin in 1924. Its members vowed then that they would learn to live, work and fight the Leninist way. This was a vow of fidelity by all Komsomol members thereafter to Lenin's behests, to the cause of the Communist Party, to the ideals of communism.

The Komsomol regards as its central tasks the fostering of ideologically committed, courageous fighters for the communist cause. It actively helps the Party to educate the younger generation in the spirit of Marxism–Leninism and the revolutionary, combat and labor traditions of the Communist Party and the Soviet people, in the spirit of readiness to defend, arms in hand, the gains of the Great October Socialist Revolution.

The Komsomol uses a wide variety of forms for the ideological and political education of youth. About 20 million young workers, collective farmers and specialists have experienced the system of Party and Komsomol political education or the system of mass economic education. Most students take part in annual all-Union reviews of compositions on sociopolitical subjects and student essay competitions on topics concerning social science, the history of the Komsomol and the international youth movement. An important place in the ideological and political education of our youth is occupied by what we call Lenin lessons and Lenin tests, which help them in their study of Lenin's theoretical works and cultivate in them an activist attitude to life.

Warm support is given by Soviet youth to the All-Union March to Places of Revolutionary, Combat and Labor Glory. Millions of young men and women take part in it and come to know better the heroic history of the Soviet people, the exploits of their parents and grandparents, and they learn to appreciate the people who have given much of their strength and health to the struggle for the happiness of our country.

With dedication the Komsomol carries out Lenin's behest:

"Only by working side by side with the workers and peasants can one become a genuine Communist."[1] Komomol construction projects have become a real school of life for hundreds of thousands of young men and women. In 1980 alone, 125,000 young volunteers went to work on such projects. After the Twenty-fifth Congress of the CPSU a mass movement under the motto "Youthful Enthusiasm and Initiative for the Five-Year Plan of Efficiency and Quality" got under way.

It has become a tradition to hold all-union reviews of scientific and technical creative work done by young people, in which almost 20 million young men and women are regularly engaged.

Important work is conducted by the Komsomol in training and educating a worthy reserve for the working class and the collective-farm peasantry, in exercising patronage over vocational schools and sending young people to work in sectors of the economy where there is a shortage of manpower, such as the services industry, livestock breeding and others.

A considerable contribution is made by students and pupils to the national economy. In the summer of 1980 the all-union student building detachment did work worth more than 1,500 million rubles, and more than 10 million senior school students worked on collective and state farms and in industrial enterprises.

An important aspect of the Komsomol work is active assistance to the Party in molding a harmoniously developed younger generation. Komsomol organizations encourage young workers, collective farmers and office employees to enroll in evening and correspondence schools, specialized secondary schools, institutes and universities. Millions of Komsomol members and other young people enjoy physical culture, sports and the arts as hobbies.

The Komsomol shows special concern for schoolchildren. Komsomol organizations take an active part in improving methods of instruction and upbringing, helping students to acquire a deep knowledge of the subjects they study and preparing them

[1] V.I. Lenin, *Collected Works*, Vol. 31, p. 298.

for socially useful work and for choosing a profession or trade they really want.

The Party has given the Komsomol extensive rights for the performance of its functions. It actively participates in the formation of representative bodies of state authority, in initiating legislation, in control over the observance of labor laws, in the education, material maintenance and the provision of cultural facilities to young people.

As said earlier, today one in every four deputies to the USSR Supreme Soviet, one in every five deputies to the Supreme Soviets of the union republics and one in every three deputies to local Soviets is under 30 years of age. In recent years the Komsomol Central Committee has adopted a number of resolutions on strengthening ties with the Soviets of People's Deputies, working more with young deputies and enhancing their role in the organs of powers.

Many young deputies are members of the Soviets' standing commissions on youth affairs. Not infrequently Komsomol workers are elected chairmen of these commissions, which, jointly with Komsomol bodies, consider questions of the work, education and recreation of young people and submit relevant proposals to the Soviets and their executive committees.

The Komsomol widely uses its constitutional right to initiate legislation. After the 18th Congress of the Komsomol (April 1978) the Komsomol Central Committee, jointly with state and public organizations, adopted more than 560 resolutions on questions relating to the work, study and recreation of young people. Komsomol organizations take an active part in the discussion of the most important pieces of draft legislation and in the drafting of directives directly bearing on the interests of youth.

Representatives of the Komsomol sit on the boards of many ministries and departments dealing with the upbringing and education of youth and take an active part in managing socialist production. About two million young workers have been elected to leading trade-union bodies and local trade-union committees. Young people make up one-third of trade union group organizers. Komsomol functionaries and activists are included in standing production committees.

Komsomol organizations actively exercise their right to take part in considering questions of awarding bonuses to young employees, of providing them with apartments or accommodations in dormitories, of protecting adolescent labor, of the hiring and dismissal of young workers and questions concerning the use of funds allocated for mass cultural and sporting activities. They also take part in drafting and implementing collective agreements and plans for the social development of work collectives.

Recently such public bodies as young workers' and specialists' councils, public personnel departments, bureaus of economic analysis and technical information, design and technological bureaus and many others have become increasingly active.

The Komsomol has been entrusted by the Communist Party with the task of guiding the All-Union Young Pioneer Organization named after Lenin, which unites about 19 million children. Set up in 1922, the Young Pioneer Organization, together with the school, the family and the public, brings up its members as conscientious fighters for the cause of the Communist Party. It instills in them love for work and knowledge and inculcates in them elementary skills and habits of social work. In the Young Pioneer groups children are educated in the spirit of collectivism and comradeship, love for the Soviet homeland, fraternal friendship for the peoples of the USSR and proletarian internationalism.

Komsomol members are assigned posts as Young Pioneer detachments leaders and heads of various hobby circles. The highest governing body of the All-Union Young Pioneer Organization is the Central Council, which is formed by the Komsomol Central Committee.

The most important aspect of the work of the Komsomol is to help mold a generation of people who are politically active, competent, industrious and always ready to stand up in defense of the country. This was again stressed in the decisions of the 26th Congress of the CPSU. The Party believes that to reliably guarantee that Soviet youth will always carry the banner of communism high, it must pass on to them its experience and its convictions that Marxism–Leninism is correct, a conviction that has stood the test of many decades.

An important role in the life of Soviet society is played by cooperative and especially by collective farms. There were 26,000 collective farms at the beginning of 1980. They united 13.8 million Soviet farmers.

Before the Great October Socialist Revolution, two-thirds of the country's peasantry were poor peasants dependent on estate owners and rich villagers, (kulaks). Soviet government abolished private land ownership. The peasants received for their use, free of charge, more than 150 billion hectares[1] of land that formerly belonged to landowners, the bourgeoisie, the royal family, the churches and monasteries. They were exempted from paying rent and freed from the expense of purchasing the land. "In this peasant country," Lenin wrote, "it was the peasantry . . . who were the first to gain, who gained most and gained immediately from the dictatorship of the proletariat."[2]

Lenin regarded cooperation with peasants in production and radical socioeconomic changes in the entire way of life in the countryside as stepping stones to socialism and communism. The cooperative plan elaborated by Lenin became the basis of the Party's agrarian policy. The plan, based on the ideas of Marx and Engels, consisted of gradually turning small peasant holdings into collective farms; it took into consideration the specific features of our country and the experience of the first collective farms in the Soviet countryside.

Communists realized that it would be impossible to carry out the transition to large-scale collective farming immediately after the revolution, and not only because the material and technical prerequisites for that were lacking. The peasants who had received land needed time to shed the age-old, small-proprietor mentality and to become convinced of the advantages of collective farming. "We did not want to impose on the peasants the

---

[1] One hectare equals 2.471 acres.
[2] V.I. Lenin, *Collected Works*, Vol. 30, p. 112.

idea that the equal division of land was useless, an idea which was alien to them," Lenin said. "Far better, we thought if, by their own experience and suffering, the peasants themselves come to realize that equal division is nonsense . . . The solution lies only in socialized farming."[1] Practice bore out the correctness of this policy.

By the end of the 1920s small individual holdings had almost exhausted their possibilities. They were no longer able to ensure the further growth of production. Not only the poor peasants, but also the "middle" ones came to see that individual farming had no future. In the meantime, the state was doing everything to strengthen the few production cooperatives that existed then, giving them tax concessions, supplying them with machines, etc. It was rapidly building larger tractor and combine harvester plants and setting up an industry to make agricultural machinery. Consumers' and artisans' cooperatives became widespread in the countryside, and peasants got accustomed to running things collectively. The socialist sector was expanding and gaining strength. Two poles were taking shape, with the poor peasants and most of the middle ones at one end and the kulaks at the other.

In such conditions a plenary meeting in November 1929 of the Party's Central Committee announced a course of mass-scale collectivization of agriculture. It said that, when carrying out this policy, the strictest account should be taken of the level of economic and cultural development of different regions of the country.

Poor peasants willingly joined collective farms. They were followed by many peasants having larger holdings, but the more well-to-do part of the peasantry came out against the very idea of collective farming. They began to destroy the property of collective farms and to commit terrorist acts against Party and government officials and collective farm activists.

On January 30, 1930, the Central Committee of the Party adopted a resolution "On Measures to Liquidate Kulak Holdings in Areas of Total Collectivization." The propositions of

[1]V.I. Lenin, *Collected Works*, Vol. 28, p. 175.

these decisions were incorporated in legislative acts. A differentiated approach to the kulaks was used during their implementation. Organizers of armed actions were to be isolated from society. The most troublesome kulaks were resettled in remote and sparsely populated areas and the rest, in regions outside the collective farms but within the same regions, territories and republics.

To implement the program of socialist transformations in agriculture, 2,500 Party functionaries, more than 27,000 industrial workers and many specialists were sent to the countryside. The state allocated considerable funds as well as large quantities of machines for the program. All this imparted a wide scope to the collective farm movement.

Alongside great successes, collectivization was attended by errors in its initial stage. The transformation of tens of millions of individual peasant holdings into collective farms had no precedent. The organizers lacked experience and tended to underestimate the strength of the attachment of the middle peasant to individual farming. In some places the principle of voluntary participation was not observed and specific local conditions were not taken into account. In this connection the 16th Party Congress (June–July 1930) said: "Collective farms can be built only on the basis of voluntary participation. Any attempt to use coercion or administrative compulsion with regard to the masses of poor and middle peasants with the aim of joining them to collectives is a gross violation of the Party's line and an abuse of power."

By the end of 1931, 62 percent of peasant holdings had joined collective farms, and by 1937 the socialist transformation of agriculture had been completed. Now collective farms united 93 percent of peasant households and over 99 percent of the areas already under crops.

The socialist sector became predominant in the countryside; the division of the peasantry into poor peasants, middle peasants and kulaks was abolished, and there came into being a new, socialist class—the collective farm peasantry.

It now became possible to carry out farming on an industrial basis, using the achievements of science; collective farms ensured the peasantry a prosperous life and a steady rise in their educational and cultural levels.

"The idea of the great Lenin on cooperation and the policy of the Party in solving the peasant question have fully withstood the test of time," Leonid Brezhnev said. "The experience of the USSR and other socialist countries demonstrates with utmost clarity that the building of socialism in the countryside is the peasantry's only way to happiness, is the basis for the well-being of all the working people."

An active role is played in the life of our country by other public organizations, such as consumers' and house-building cooperatives, scientific, technical, educational, sports and defense societies, professional unions, book lovers' societies, societies for the protection of nature, hunters' and anglers' societies, etc. In all, there are about 7,000 all-union, republican and local voluntary groups. Popular mass movements are represented by the Soviet Women's Committee, the Soviet Peace Committee, the Soviet War Veterans' Committee and others. The scope of public organizations widens constantly, extending their influence to practically the entire population of the country. Each of them operates on a broad democratic basis, freely considering and deciding matters relating to their activities.

The greater the activity of these organizations, the greater their contribution to communist construction. Therefore the Party is directly interested in enhancing their role in the life of society and enabling them to apply their strengths and possibilities more fully.

FRIENDSHIP AND FRATERNITY OF PEOPLES

> Citizens of the USSR of different races and nationalities have equal rights. From Article 36 of the USSR Constitution

There are more than 100 nations and nationalities in our country, whose numbers range from 137 million Russians to 504 Negidaltsi, an ethnic group in the Soviet Far East. All of them, in accordance with the Constitution, have equal rights.

Communists have always viewed the national question through the prism of socioeconomic relations, through the prism of class struggle. This was definitely stated already in the *Communist Manifesto,* written by Marx and Engels, "In proportion as the antagonism between classes within the nation vanishes, the hostility of one nation to another will come to an end."[1]

The ideas of the founders of scientific communism were creatively developed by Lenin. In an epoch when imperialism had aggravated national contradictions in the extreme, Lenin evolved the theory of the national question, explained the role of the struggle for national liberation and elaborated the scientific principles of the Communist Party's national policy.

Lenin discovered the law of two opposing tendencies in the national question under capitalism. "Developing capitalism," he wrote, "knows two historical tendencies in the national question. The first is the awakening of national life and national movements, the struggle against all national oppression and the creation of national states. The second is the development and growing frequency of international intercourse in every form, the breakdown of national barriers, the creation of the international unity of capital, of economic life in general, of politics, science, etc."[2]

[1] Karl Marx, Frederick Engels, *Collected Works,* Vol. 6, p. 503.
[2] V.I. Lenin, *Collected Works,* Vol. 20, p. 27.

Under imperialism there is irreconcilable contradiction between the two tendencies, with the internationalization of socio-economic life taking the form not of cooperation among equal nations, but of the subjugation, as in prerevolutionary Russia, of less developed nations by more developed ones. This inevitably gives rise to resistance on the part of the subjugated peoples. That is why, along with the unifying tendency, there is the tendency toward the destruction of the compulsory forms of this union.

Czarist Russia was called a prison house of nations. The czarist government's policy was aimed not only at oppressing peoples, but also at inciting national enmity and hatred.

Our Party believed that to solve the national question in Russia it was necessary, first of all to unite the working people, irrespective of nationality, in a common struggle for a new social system. However, such a union could be strong only if it were based on voluntary participation and the mutual trust of all nations. For this reason the Communists came out first of all for the right of all nations to self-determination, to secession, to the formation of independent states. As Lenin explained, ". . . we do so not because we *favor secession,* but *only* because we stand for *free, voluntary* association and merging as distinct from forcible association. That is the *only* reason."[1]

For the peoples who wished to remain within the framework of a single state, the Party called for the broadest autonomy, the enactment of special laws which would guarantee the free development of national minorities, full equality of citizens irrespective of race and nationality, the right of every citizen to address meetings in his or her native language, the introduction of local language alongside the language used throughout the state in all local public and state institutions, etc.

This position was conducive to the growth of the influence of Communists among the non-Russian peoples of Russia, to the merging of the national liberation movement with the social struggle of the workers and peasants and, in the final count, to the victory of Soviet power in the borderlands of Russia. This

[1]V.I. Lenin, *Collected Works,* Vol. 23, p. 67.

put an end to old national enmity and formed the basis on which, immediately after the revolution, the movement for the association of the peoples in a free union emerged.

The Great October Socialist Revolution became the main political factor in implementing Lenin's national program. On October 25, 1917, the 2nd All-Russia Congress of Soviets had already solemnly proclaimed, in the appeal "To Workers, Peasants, and Soldiers!," that Soviet power would guarantee a genuine right to self-determination to all the peoples of Russia. The congress formed the Council of People's Commissars (the government), within the framework of which the People's Commissariat (ministry) for the Affairs of Nationalities was established. A week later the government's Declaration of Rights of the Peoples of Russia proclaimed the equality and sovereignty of the peoples of Russia; their right to free self-determination up to secession and the formation of an independent state; the abolition of all national and national-religious privileges and restrictions; and the free development of national minorities and ethnic groups.

In December 1917, the Soviet Government recognized the state independence of the Ukraine and Finland. There began to emerge on the territory of the former Russian Empire independent Soviet republics—the Russian (established as an open federation), Ukrainian, then Azerbaijanian, Armenian and Georgian Soviet republics. There also appeared autonomous state formations of different peoples. Lenin regarded the creation of the national statehood of the peoples of our country as one of the greatest gains of the October Revolution.

The monarchists, liberals and socialists said then that the Bolsheviks were demolishing the Russian state, that all nationalities were running away from them. In reality, it was the bourgeois nationalists, not the Communists, who were working for the dismemberment of Russia; whereas prior to the revolution they had stood for "one indivisible" bourgeois Russia and sought only internal autonomy, after the victory of the revolution they sought to bring about the splitting up of the former Russian Empire into separate bourgeois states.

The Communist Party guided the liberation movement of the

peoples. With the utmost patience and circumspection, it led the masses in the practical implementation of the task of creating a single federal, multinational Soviet state.

In the initial period, when the working people of different nationalities first became aware of their independent identity, their cooperation did not yet have definite forms. But in the Civil War and in the face of foreign military intervention, it took the form of a close military, political alliance. The pooling of economic and military resources ensured victory over internal and external counterrevolution. Subsequently the military alliance was supplemented with an economic alliance. In 1920–1921 these relations between independent Soviet republics were formalized in a number of treaties.

At the same time, the tasks of safeguarding the gains of the revolution against internal and external enemies, of putting an end to economic dislocation and of building socialism made it ever more necessary that the Soviet republics should unite to form a single state. In the conditions of hostile capitalist encirclement, none of them could feel safe when separated from the others. The Russian Soviet Federative Socialist Republic became the rallying point. It has the largest centers of industry and culture. It was giving military, political, diplomatic, economic and cultural assistance to the other Soviet republics. At that time it was the world's only state with experience in organizing peaceful coexistence and cooperation among so many nations and nationalities. Drawing on this experience, the 10th Party Congress (March 1921) stated in its resolution on the national question: "A federation of Soviet republics based on a community of military and economic interests is the general form of state union which makes it possible: a) to ensure the integrity and economic development of both individual republics and of the federation as a whole; b) to embrace all the variety of customs, culture and economic conditions of thm different nations and nationalities that are at different stages of development, and accordingly to apply various forms of federation; c) to organize peaceful coexistence and fraternal cooperation of the nations and nationalities which have, in one form or another, linked their destiny with that of the federation."

On December 30, 1922, on the basis of free expression of the will of the peoples, the 1st All-Union Congress of Soviets proclaimed the establishment of the Union of Soviet Socialist Republics (the USSR). The first Constitution of the USSR, adopted in 1924, legislatively affirmed the union of the Soviet republics into a single multinational state on the basis of their sovereignty and full equality. The entire subsequent experience of the Soviet national-state system corroborated the vitality of these principles. "The Union of Soviet Socialist Republics," it is stated in the 1977 Constitution of the USSR, "is an integral, federal, multinational state formed on the princple of socialist federalism as a result of the free self-determination of nations and the voluntary association of equal Soviet Socialist Republics."

It should be noted in this connection that, as distinct from the Soviet Union, bourgeois federations were established not on the basis of the free expression of the will of their members, but through compulsion, by frequently overcoming the resistance of some of the constituent states and sometimes by acquiring territory through various means (conquest, purchase, etc.). As a rule, they represent the administrative unification of territories not connected with the national composition of the population or with the borders within which the separate nationalities live. For example, there are 50 states in the United States of America, but not more than seven basic national groups. At the same time, the indigenous population, the Indians, have no national-state formation of their own.

Exercising the right to self-determination, the numerous nations and nationalities of our country created different forms of national statehood. At present these are union and autonomous republics and autonomous regions and areas. As years went by, the number of state-national organizations increased. In 1924, there were 4 union republics, 13 autonomous republics and 13 autonomous regions; today the USSR is comprised of 15 union republics, 20 autonomous republics, 8 autonomous regions and 10 autonomous areas.

The USSR as a federal state is formed on the principle of democratic centralism, which makes it possible to combine most effectively the common interests of all the peoples of the country with the national interests of the constituent republics. Centralism has to do with the basic questions of governing the country as a whole; it is necessary owing to the requirements of the socialist economy and the interests of the sociopolitical and intellectual development of society and of the country's defense. But it operates in organic interconnection with democracy, with the broad autonomy of the republics, with the unimpeded development of their initiative.

In accordance with the USSR Constitution, all the union republics are sovereign Soviet socialist states. This means that they retain their independence and autonomy in exercising state power in all areas of political, economic, cultural and social life with the exception of those which, by the general consent of the republics, come within the jurisdiction of the USSR Supreme Soviet and the government of the USSR.

The sovereign rights of the union republics are securely guaranteed. Each of them has its own Constitution, which conforms with the Constitution of the USSR and takes into account the specific national features of the republic, and its own citizenship. Each republic independently decides questions relating to the administrative-territorial setup and has the right to enter into relations with foreign states. The territory of a union republic cannot be altered without its consent. Each union republic retains the right to secede from the USSR.

The Supreme Soviet of a union republic is its only legislative body which is empowered to deal with all matters within the jurisdiction of the union republic under the Constitution of the USSR and the constitution of the union republic.

In some union republics, in addition to the nationality that has given its name to the republic, there live other peoples or ethnic groups. They have national–territorial autonomy at different levels.

An autonomous republic is a Soviet socialist state which is a part of a union republic. It has its own constitution, and the right, within the sphere of its jurisdiction, to issue laws which accord with the Constitution and laws of the USSR and those of the union republic of which it is a part; it has its own supreme bodies of state authority and administration, and its own citizenship. The territory of an autonomous republic cannot be altered without its consent.

An autonomous region, too, forms a part of a union republic. It enjoys self-government in its internal affairs and has its own national bodies of state authority and government: the regional Soviet of People's Deputies and its executive committee.

An autonomous area is the form of Soviet statehood of the national minorities of the Soviet Far North. It ensures their administrative self-government and provides them with local national bodies of state authority and government: the area Soviets and their executive committees. An autonomous area is a part of a territory or region.

The rights of an autonomous region or area are defined by the laws of the union republic of which it is a part.

The Soviet Union is formed on the principle of equality of the union republics irrespective of the size of their population or territory, the economic development level or any other factors.

The USSR Supreme Soviet ensures the equality of the republics. It consists of two chambers, the Soviet of the Union and the Soviet of Nationalities. They have equal numbers of deputies. In the Soviet of Nationalities each union republic is represented by 32 deputies, each autonomous republic by 11 deputies, each autonomous region by five deputies, and each autonomous area by one deputy.

National equality is enforced also by the fact that every union republic has the right to take part in decision-making in the Supreme Soviet of the USSR, in its Presidium, in the Council of Ministers (government) of the USSR and in other bodies of the USSR in matters that come within the jurisdiction of the USSR. The union republics have the right to initiate legislation. They are represented in the Presidium of the USSR Supreme Soviet (the Presidium has 15 vice chairmen, one from each union republic) and in other union bodies. All the autonomous republics, regions and areas are represented in the Supreme Soviets of the corresponding union republics depending on the size of their population. The representative of an Autonomous Republic is a vice chairman of the Supreme Soviet of the union republic of which it is a part.

Citizens of the USSR have an equal right under the law to use their native languages and the languages of other peoples of the Country in school, in the press, on the radio and TV. Laws of the USSR, decisions and other acts of the USSR Supreme Soviet are published in the languages of the union republics. This principle is also strictly observed in the judiciary.

Violation of national equality involves criminal and other liability. As is stated in the Constitution of the USSR, any direct of indirect limitation of the right of citizens of establishment of direct or indirect privileges on grounds of race or nationality, as well as any advocacy of racial or national exclusiveness, hostility or contempt, are punishable by law. "It is the duty of every citizen of the USSR," the Constitution says, "to respect the national dignity of other citizens, and to strengthen friendship of the nations and nationalities of the multinational Soviet state."

The legal equality established in the very first days of Soviet government did not mean the immediate solution of the national question. It was necessary to do away with actual inequality, to overcome the economic and cultural backwardness of the formerly oppressed nations and nationalities. This required much time. Back in 1921, the 10th Party Congress pointed out that "the abolition of actual national inequality is a long process, requiring a determined struggle against all the remnants of oppression and colonial slavery."

The Party pursued a course of accelerated economic, cultural and social development of the national borderlands: Kazakhstan, Central Asia, the Caucasus and the North.

This policy was founded on a firm conviction that economic equality is the basis of actual equality. The formation of the USSR opened up broad possibilities for the accomplishment of this task, which was to concentrate the material resources of the republics and use them to create bases of production where they did not exist before, establish economic ties between various regions, organize exchange of experience and send specialists to areas where they were needed. Within 10 to 12 years, thanks to the efforts of all the peoples of the USSR, a modern industry, heavy industry in the first place, was built. Productive forces were distributed with account taken of the requirements both of the country as a whole and of the national borderlands.

Large-scale development of natural riches and construction of industrial complexes were launched in Soviet Central Asia, Kazakhstan, Transcaucasia, Siberia, the Soviet Far East, the Urals and the Volga area, i.e., regions whose population in the past consisted largely of oppressed nations and nationalities.

The decisive role in the accelerated economic development of the republics of Soviet Central Asia, Transcaucasia and Kazakhstan was played by the material, political and organizational assistance rendered by the working class and all working people of the developed regions of the USSR. This disinterested assistance was given within the framework of a nationwide economic policy worked out by the Party. Vast sums were allocated for the implementation of land and water reform in Soviet Central Asia, for helping the nomads change over to a settled way of life. The Russian working class and the entire Russian people made sacrifices in order to help do away with the backwardness of the national borderlands, regarding this as their internationalist duty. Thus, while in the Russian Federation gross industrial output grew six times between 1928 and 1940, the increase in Kazakhstan and Georgia was eight times, in Tajikistan and Armenia, nine times, and in Kirghizia, ten times.

Elimination of the cultural backwardness of the formerly oppressed peoples was regarded by the Party as one of the central tasks in solving the national question. Again, this task could be accomplished only given all-round assistance and high rates of cultural development. Within a very short space of time, mass illiteracy was eradicated in the national regions. A ramified network of secondary, specialized secondary and higher schools, libraries, clubhouses and research establishments were built there. The central regions sent technical specialists, doctors, teachers and cultural workers. Additional funds were allocated to meet the needs of health protection and education. National personnel were given special privileges for enrolling in higher educational establishments.

It should be specially noted that one of the greatest achievements of socialism is the unbreakable friendship of the peoples of the USSR. This friendship, in which we justly take pride, is the result of overcoming what was left of an epoch of national oppression, shown in great-power chauvinism, a reflection of the former privileged position of the Russian nationality, and manifestations of nationalism among some peoples who had not been freed from the effects of old national injuries. Both these phenomena hampered the actual unification of the republics into a single state union.

The Party combatted the nationalist survivals, above all great-power chauvinism. Rallying the working people under the motto of proletarian internationalism, it called for a considerate attitude toward the national feelings of every people. The Party pointed out in its Second Program (1919): "The proletariat of the former oppressor nations should display special caution and special attention to the remnants of national feelings among the working people of the formerly oppressed or unequal nations." The Great Patriotic War of 1941–1945 against Nazi Germany became a grueling test of the strength of the multinational Soviet state. As it prepared for war, the Nazis expected a revival of national strife in the Soviet Union. Hermann Göring's "Green File" enjoined Nazi officers: "In the Baltic countries use, in the interests of Germany, conflicts between the Lithuanians, Estonians, Letts and Russians . . . In the South, conflicts between the Ukrainians and the Russians . . . In the Caucasus, conflicts between the natives: the Georgians and the Armenians, and the Georgians and the Russians."

This plan was never to be realized. Far from weakening in the face of danger, the friendship of the Soviet peoples grew stronger and became one of the principal factors of the Soviet Union's victory over Hitlerite fascism. Members of all the peoples and nationalities of our country fought on the fronts of the Great Patriotic War, upholding their freedom and independence.

Today the national question, in the form in which it existed before the revolution, has been fully resolved. There is no question of eliminating national oppression, inequality and antagonism any longer. "This is an accomplishment," Leonid Brezhnev said, "which can by rights be ranked on a par with the victories in building the new society in the USSR, such as industrialization, collectivization and the cultural revolution."

Of course, not all questions in the sphere of national relations have been solved. The dynamics of the development of such a large multinational state as the USSR gives rise to many problems requiring the tact and attention of the Party. The CPSU, it was stressed at the 26th Congress, has fought and will always fight against such attitudes that are alien to socialism as chauvinism or nationalism, against any nationalistic aberration, be it anti-Semitism or Zionism. The survivals of the past, regrettably, still manifest themselves from time to time. These attitudes have a history of many centuries, and, moreover, Western propaganda is trying to revive them. While we are against attempts to artificially obliterate specific national features, we are equally against attempts to artificially inflate their significance. The Party regards it as a sacred duty to educate the people in a spirit of Soviet patriotism and socialist internationalism, to foster in them a sense of pride in belonging to the great integral Soviet Motherland.

Strict observance of the provisions of the Constitution, full utilization of the mechanisms ensuring equal participation of all nations and nationalities in dealing with matters of common interest and, of course, Leninist tact in deciding all matters, however insignificant they may seem to be, that have a bearing on the national question. The experience of past decades helps us implement this policy. This experience, not only the principles, enables us to avoid excesses and helps us to harmoniously combine international and national interests. We clearly see and enthusiastically welcome the drawing together of the Soviet peoples, which is an objective process, a leading trend of development of our country, peoples, and we also welcome the growth and multiplication of everything arising from life within a single state, under a single social system. Alongside this we see the full richness of the national life of each people, the development of its forms, the blossoming of culture. This is a twofold, interconnected process. By freely communicating with one another as friends and coming closer together, the peoples enrich one another with what is specifically national and mold what we call a new community of peoples—the Soviet people.

EMANCIPATION OF WOMEN

> Women and men have equal rights in the USSR. From Article 35 of the USSR Constitution.

The level of culture and maturity of a society can be judged by the position the woman occupies in it.

In prerevolutionary Russia, there were laws under which a wife could not obtain a passport, acquire property, enter the civil service or change her place of residence without the permission of her husband. Domestic servants and farmhands made up 80 percent of the total number of women working for wages; only 13 percent worked in industry and construction and 4 percent in educational and medical establishments. Only 11 in a thousand women had more than an elementary education. "We gave birth between looms. The terrible threat of dismissal and hunger hung constantly over our heads," it was said in a letter sent by the spinners and weavers of the Trekhgornaya (formerly Prokhorov's) textile mills to the Party's Central Committee in the 1930s.

Lenin regarded struggle for the emancipation of women as an organic part of the cause of the working class: "The proletariat cannot achieve complete liberty until it has won complete liberty for women."[1] This was best understood by women workers. "We would not have won without them. Or would scarcely have won,"[2] said Lenin.

In the very first months of its existence Soviet power annulled the old laws that placed women in a subordinate position. The decrees on civil marriage and divorce abolished inequality in marriage and family law. Equality of political and civil rights and equal pay for equal work were established for men and women. A social insurance system was introduced envisaging paid leaves for expectant mothers. The equality of the political and civil rights of men and women proclaimed by the revolution was given legal force in the first Constitution of the Soviet Republic.

However, equality under the law did not yet mean equality in actual life. The main problem in the first years was to encourage as many women as possible to do socially useful work. It was also important to raise their political awareness, their cultural and educational levels and to free them from "domestic slavery."

The Party's Second Program became the first program in history attempting to solve the problem of feminine equality. Specifically it set the task of destroying, with the help of ideological and educational work, all traces of past inequality and prejudices against women, especially among the backward strata of the proletariat and the peasantry, and to free women from the burden of housekeeping by building communal houses, public dining halls, communal laundries, nurseries, etc.

The Party sought new forms and methods of work to help women workers and peasant women to really exercise the rights granted to them by the revolution. It organized all-Russia and all-Union women's congresses, rallies, conferences and meetings in regions, territories and national republics. The Central Committee and, after that, all the regional, territorial and district committees of the Party set up commissions for work among women, which were later reorganized into women's departments.

[1] V.I. Lenin, *Collected Works*, Vol. 30. p. 372.
[2] Clara Zetkin, *My Recollections of Lenin,* Foreign Languages Publishing House, Moscow, 1956, p. 54.

These departments held meetings, conferences and congresses and published leaflets, pamphlets, magazines and the special series "The Woman Worker's and Peasant Library". They took part in the discussion of draft laws bearing on the interests of women, initiated many government resolutions and submitted proposals during consideration of budgets and plans for the development of the national economy.

There emerged a new form of public activity—standing delegates' assemblies. The delegates were elected at meetings of woman workers, peasant women and housewives. In 1926, for instance, 620,000 delegates were elected, and in 1927, 747,000.

The program of delegates' assemblies included lectures on political subjects and discussion of questions pertaining to the activities of local Soviets, cooperatives, trade unions and various economic agencies. Delegates were sent for practical training to institutions dealing with questions of labor, public education, public health, food supply and social security. As instructors they took part in considering complaints and requests, in receiving visitors in offices and in exercising control over the work of various departments. The most capable of the delegates stayed on as permanent employes where they had received practical training.

After the revolution a network of mother and child care institutions was established. Already in 1922, despite the famine and the economic dislocation, there were 300 women's consultation centers and children's outpatient clinics. Nursing mothers received allowances, and free meals were provided to children.

The first step toward a new life were particularly difficult for the women of the East, where such patriarchal-tribal and feudal relations and customs still survived as polygamy, the sale and purchase of brides, the marrying of minors, etc. Women's clubs (including traveling ones for the nomads), were set up there. These were institutions of a special kind: In addition to literacy courses, libraries and amateur art groups, they included legal aid bureaus, medical consultation centers, nurseries and kindergartens and production workshops. The emancipation of the women of the East demanded perserverance and much effort by the Party to overcome the fierce resistance of fanatics. To get an idea of the acuteness and complexity of the problem, let us turn to several reports from *Pravda* in October 1927, at a time when the country was preparing to mark the 10th anniversary of the socialist revolution.

Here are some excerpts from these reports.

"The life of women in the East was a nightmare, and many traces of the feminine slavery of the past remain part of everyday life to this day. In many districts people still have to learn what soap is, and many women become invalids after childbirth . . . Women are often looked upon as creatures of a lower order. Backward customs often prevent them from getting an education on a par or together with men . . .

"In 1927, 90,000 women in Uzbekistan threw away the veil . . . The whole reactionary world of mullahs, landowners and kulaks took up the cudgels against them . . . Women delegates conducting propaganda and organizational work among women are persecuted by fanatics to the extent of being savagely beaten and murdered by them . . . But there is no return to the past. The woman slave of yesterday is now as much the master of the Soviet country as all working people."

The Communist Party undertook great efforts to involve women in social production, the basis of their actual equality and economic independence. In the first years of Soviet power this question was given special attention at a number of Party congresses.

Besides other factors, the difficulty of the problem lay in the fact that the building of socialism in our country began in conditions of economic dislocation and unemployment caused by the Civil War and foreign military intervention. Nevertheless, everything possible was done to secure the participation of women in social production. The 13th Party Congress (1924) pointed out that "the retaining of a female labor force in production has a political significance and places before the Party the task of intensifying the work of raising the qualifications of female workers and attracting women, where possible, to those branches of production in which female labor was not used at all or was used insufficiently." Later on a special five-year plan for drawing women into social production was worked out. Between 1929 and 1936, the number of women factory and office workers in the national economy rose by more than five million.

By the end of the 1930s there was complete literacy among women working in industry. The professional and technical background of young men and women workers had been made more equal thanks to the establishment of a mandatory percentage of young women admitted into factory schools.

The position of peasant women underwent profound changes following collectivization. Cooperatives, as public organizations in which women participate on an equal basis with men, helped assert their actual equality.

The measures conducted in the country to secure the participation of women in socialist construction eliminated the vast gap between the social position of men and women. Increasing activity on the part of working women helped to multiply the successes of socialism, and each new success was a further step toward women's actual emancipation. The 1936 Constitution of the USSR summarized the achievements in resolving the woman question, granted to women equal rights with men in all spheres of economic, state, cultural and sociopolitical life and gave guarantees of these rights.

In defining the principal tasks of communist construction, recent Party congresses called for the complete elimination of the vestiges of the unequal position of women in everyday life, for the creation of social and everyday conditions enabling women to combine motherhood with ever more vigorous participation in social labor and public activities, in scientific and artistic pursuits. The country's great economic successes made it possible to carry out a new, extensive program of social undertakings. All this was included in the 1977 Constitution of the USSR.

Among the most important guarantees of women's equality is the provision to women of equal opportunities in employment, pay and promotion. This is understandable. It is women's participation in socially useful labor that creates a real basis for the actual equality of women with men.

The Soviet Union has the highest level of employment of

women in the world. Women make up more than half of all wage-earning and salaried workers in the country, and there are more women working in industry, including those branches that require highly qualified personnel, than in any other sector of the economy.

Profound qualitative changes are taking place in the countryside. The number of women drivers of farm machines and operators of automated poultry factories and mechanized livestock complexes is growing.

There has been a rapid increase in the number of women engaged primarily in intellectual labor. The number of women specialists with a higher or secondary specialized education is more than 16.4 million, or 58 percent of the total. Women account for almost half of the number of engineers in industry and about 40 percent of agronomists, livestock experts and veterinary surgeons. Women play a leading role in health protection and education, accounting for two-thirds of the physicians and almost three-quarters of the teachers. More than half a million women are managers of industrial enterprises, state farms, construction projects, trading establishments, health protection, public catering and communal service establishments, and heads of administrative bodies.

Women make up about 40 percent of the country's scientific workers. They take an active part in research in thermonuclear synthesis, space biology, mathematical physics, genetics, the chemistry of high-molecular compounds, and radio engineering. About 116,100 women hold degrees of candidate and doctor of sciences; among academicians, corresponding members of the USSR Academy of Sciences and professors, 2,900 are women.

It may be noted, by way of comparison, that in the mid-seventies in the United States women constituted 1.1 percent of engineers, seven percent of doctors, and less than one percent of physicists and mathematicians. The official figures show that 80 percent of working women in the United States are employed at low paid, low skilled jobs. A similar situation exists in other capitalist countries. Unemployment is notoriously much higher among women than among men in the capitalist world.

Soviet legislation rules out any discrimination of women in pay. The wage rates and salaries are the same for men and women of the same qualification in all branches of the national economy. Moreover, Soviet legislation provides for a number of concessions and privileges for working women. For instance, women transferred to lighter jobs because of pregnancy retain the average earnings they received at their previous jobs. The work quotas for women farm-machinery operators is ten percent lower than for men, while receiving the same wages as the latter.

In the United States, female labor is paid much less than male labor, and the gap constantly widens. In 1956, women working full time received 63.9 percent of the earnings of men doing the same work; at the end of 1978, they got only 58.9 percent.

The USSR Constitution guarantees to women equal access with men to education and vocational and professional training. The doors of general, specialized secondary, vocational and higher schools are wide open before them. The curriculum for men and women is the same in all schools. In specialized secondary school women make up 56 percent of the students, and in higher schools, 52 percent. More than 800 out of every 1,000 women employed in the national economy have at least some secondary or higher education.

Let us draw some parallels in this case as well. In the 1976–77 academic year, women accounted for only 25 percent of the student body in U.S. medical schools and only 20 percent in some law schools. In France, girls are virtually excluded from many higher and vocational schools. Higher education is a male privilege in Japan.

The CPSU Central Committee and the USSR Council of Ministers pay special attention to improving the qualifications of working women. It is important to note that working women having children under eight years of age are now being re-trained or are enrolled in refresher courses, and they receive their average wages for the period of study during which they are not working.

The USSR Constitution guarantees to women equal opportunities with men in social, political and cultural activity. This is evidenced by the following data. Women constitute 49.5 percent of the deputies of the Supreme Soviets of the union and autonomous republics and local Soviets. There are 487 women deputies, almost one-third of the total, in the Supreme Soviet, the highest body of state authority, and four of them are members of its Presidium. Women head deputies' standing committees and hold important posts in the governments of the union and autonomous republics. Many women have been elected chairpersons and secretaries of the executive committees of local Soviets. Women make up 66 percent of the staff of the country's administrative agencies.

There are only 21 women in the U.S. Congress, and only two in the Senate. Women hold a little over 10 percent of elective offices, primarily in local government organs, in the United States.

The active role played by women in the CPSU should be particularly stressed. As of January 1, 1981, there were 4.6 million women members in the Party, or 26.5 percent of the total. Women constitute 21.4 percent of the secretaries of district and city Party committees and more than 35 percent of the secretaries of primary Party organizations.

In addition to other guarantees of actual equality the USSR Constitution envisages special measures for the protection of the labor and health of women. Putting women in particularly arduous jobs, those detrimental to health or involving carrying or shifting loads whose weights exceed established norms, is prohibited. In a number of trades and professions women enjoy additional benefits such as shorter working day, longer holidays and higher pensions.

Today almost 50 institutes studying the hygiene and protection of women in the work force, mothers and children and obstetrics and gynecology conduct research aimed at ensuring favorable working conditions for women and safeguarding their health.

There is strict state supervision over the observance of legislation on working women. Important work is being done in this field by the standing committees of Soviets at all levels, dealing with the question of women's working and living conditions and the protection of mothers and their children.

In the Soviet Union motherhood is regarded as the principal social function of women. *The USSR Constitution guarantees the creation of conditions enabling women to combine work with motherhood:* legal protection and material and moral support, including the provision of paid maternity leaves and other privileges and the gradual reduction of the working time of women having small children.

All working women enjoy fully paid maternity leave, regardless of seniority. The number of paid days off to look after a sick child has been increased. Low-income families receive monthly children's allowances.

On the birth of every subsequent child, mothers having two children receive a lump-sum state allowance, and those having four or more children are provided monthly children's allowances. Women who have given birth to and reared five or more children up to the age of eight may retire on pension at the age of 50 instead of 55. Mothers of many children are awarded special government decorations.

The USSR Constitution guarantees women's equality not only in work and in sociopolitical life, but also in family relations. The state helps the family by running and expanding a network of kindergartens and nurseries, organizing and improving communal services and public catering and providing various benefits for large families.

Today 14.4 million Soviet children (or every other child) attend preschool establishments. Parents contribute only 20 percent of the expenses involved, the remainder being covered by the state. Some families, especially those with many children, pay even less.

There are extended-day schools and groups where children are taken care of after classes. Their number grows steadily. At the beginning of the 1980/81 school year there were 13.2 million pupils in extended-day schools and groups, boarding schools and other institutions of this type.

There is an extensive network of children's camps. About 14 million children spent their summer in such camps in 1980. A voucher for a Young Pioneer summer camps costs the parents 12 rubles on the average, which is one-quarter of the actual cost.

There are sanatorium-type, year-round camps where children with poor health take treatment and are given instruction in accordance with the curriculum of general schools.

There is a steady increase in the number of sports and work-and-health camps for adolescents, Young Pioneer palaces and houses, young technicians' and naturalists' centers, children's clubhouses, sports and music schools and other children's establishments.

Extensive and effective measures to improve the working conditions for women, family recreation resources and everyday and cultural services to the population are outlined in the decisions of the 26th Congress of the CPSU. They include the introduction of a partially paid leave for women to look after a child until it is one year old, a shortened working day for mothers of small children, and an extension of the network and improvement of the system of preschool establishments, extended-day schools and the entire service sphere. The CPSU Central Committee and the USSR Council of Ministers have adopted a resolution "On Measures to Increase State Assistance to Families with Children".

Soviet women have advanced to a worthy place in the life of Soviet society. "When considering our people's great endeavors," Leonid Brezhnev noted, "one must also emphasize the important role which Soviet women play in them. In many ways, our homeland owes its achievements and victories to our women's dedication and talents."

PERSONAL RIGHTS AND FREEDOMS

Demands in the sphere of personal rights and freedoms of working people were put forth already in the First Program of the Party, long before the socialist revolution. They included inviolability of the person, the home, unrestricted freedom of conscience, freedom of movement and of choice of a trade or profession, and the right of every person to sue any official. The CPSU abides by these demands now as well, when it is the ruling party.

Under the Constitution of the USSR, the family enjoys the protection of the state, and citizens are guaranteed inviolability of the person and the home, protection of personal property and privacy, the right to protection of the courts and to compensations for damages, and freedom of conscience.

Respect for the individual and protection of the personal rights and freedoms of Soviet citizens is the duty of all state agencies, public organizations, officials and all citizens of the USSR.

Exercise of personal rights and freedoms in the USSR does not involve large expenditures, whereas in the West it entails considerable expenses, such as lawyer's fees, which not everybody can afford. Our laws and everyday practice rule out dependence of the exercise of rights and freedoms on the social status and financial position of citizens.

What are the legal guarantees of personal rights and freedoms in the USSR?

The constitutional right to state protection of the family is given concrete expression in a number of legislative acts and above all in the Fundamentals of the Legislation of the USSR and the Union Republics on Marriage and the Family. It is pointed out in this document that care for the family, which combines social and personal interests, is one of the most important tasks of the Soviet state.

The law recognizes only a marriage which is contracted with the free consent of the woman and the man. The Fundamentals establishes the duties of the spouses with respect to each other and to the children. Bringing up the younger generation in the spirit of communist morality is proclaimed the paramount duty of the family.

Our legislation on marriage and the family actively helps to eliminate the vestiges of the unequal position of the woman in day-to-day life.

It is often alleged in the West that Soviet citizens are not allowed to marry foreigners, that we have no freedom of emigration. The fact is that in the past few years about 10,000 Soviet citizens have married foreigners. Many of them have stayed on in the USSR, while others went to the place of residence of their husbands or wives in more than 100 countries. As for emigration, the relevant Soviet legislation and rules fully accord with the International Covenant on Civil and Political Rights, which says, among other things, that the right to go abroad may be limited in certain cases where it is necessary "to protect national security, public order, public health or morals or the rights and freedoms of others." In some cases the permission to emigrate may be postponed until the applicant's close relatives have settled their affairs, including material matters. A decision on an application for permission to emigrate may be postponed in the case of persons possessing state secrets or those who have recently undergone training in important military fields. Upon the expiration of the established time limit for secrecy, the application for emigration is reconsidered. We have no other causes for not allowing emigration.

The right to inviolability of the person means that no one may be subjected to administrative persecution or arrest except by a court decision or on the warrant of a procurator.

The detention of a person suspected of having committed a crime must be reported by the militia officer or investigator to the procurator within 24 hours. If the procurator does not give his approval for the arrest within 48 hours, the detained person must be set free. But even after the procurator has given his approval, the arrested person may be detained for only 10 days if during this time charges are not made against him of having commited a crime. Soviet criminal law establishes severe liability for illegal arrest or detention, for passing an unjust sentence, for false denunciations or making unfounded charges.

The Constitution of the USSR ensures protection of the privacy of citizens. Without lawful grounds no one has the right to enter a home against the will or without the consent of the persons residing in it, to open other people's letters and telegrams or tap telephone conversations. The state guarantees the secrecy and safekeeping of savings bank deposits. Conducting a search or examining correspondence are allowed only when, with the approval of a procurator or by a court order, and in keeping with the law, an investigation of a crime is being conducted. These constitutional provisions are backed up by other laws prescribing civil and criminal liability for their violation.

No thoughts or convictions, however reprehensible from the point of view of the authorities, involve juridical liability in the USSR. Only criminal actions are punishable. According to our criminal law, only a person who has committed a socially dangerous act as defined by the law is criminally liable and subject to punishment. The Criminal Code contains an exhaustive list of acts regarded as criminal and punishable. Soviet law allows no broad interpretation of the articles of this code.

Citizens of the USSR have the right to possess and inherit property. Their personal property may include earned savings, a house, cars and other articles of everyday use, personal consumption and convenience. They may be granted the use of plots of land by the state or by collective farms for subsidiary farming (including the keeping of livestock and poultry), for fruit and vegetable growing or for building an individual dwelling.

At present, for instance, the majority of rural residents live in their own houses and have individual plots of land. They own tens of millions of head of cattle and poultry, agricultural implements and other tools. The produce from individual plots is used for personal consumption, and the surplus is sold through procurement organizations to the state or on collective farm markets. In keeping with the Constitution, the state and the collective farms provide assistance to citizens in tending their individual plots (sale of fodder at reduced prices, assistance in the purchase of mineral fertilizers, pesticides, machinery, etc.).

In the USSR, the law permits individual labor in handicrafts, farming, the provision of services for the public and other forms of activity based exclusively on the personal work of individual citizens and members of their families.

The Constitution guarantees the right of every citizen to protection by the courts against encroachments on their life and health, personal freedom, honor and dignity, and property. Civil and criminal law provides for strict responsibility for such encroachments, no matter who makes them.

Soviet people have the right to lodge a complaint against the actions of officials and state and public agencies. Complaints are examined according to the procedure and within the time-limits established by law. Actions by officials that contravene the law or exceed their powers and infringe the rights of citizens may be appealed in court in the manner prescribed by law. Citizens have the right to compensation for damage resulting from unlawful actions by state and public organizations, or by officials in the performance of their duties.

Thus, Soviet legislation fully ensures the right to protection against arbitrary or illegal interference in the privacy of citizens.

Freedom of conscience, too, is an important constitutional guarantee of the personal rights and freedoms of Soviet people. Since the problem of religion and the church is of special interest, it merits separate consideration.

FREEDOM OF CONSCIENCE

> Citizens of the USSR are
> guaranteed freedom of
> conscience . . . From Article 52
> of the USSR Constitution

Speaking of Communists' attitude to religion, Lenin stressed: "Everyone must be absolutely free to profess any religion he pleases, or no religion whatever, i.e., to be an atheist. Discrimination among citizens on account of their religious convictions is wholly intolerable."[1]

The Marxist-Leninist principle of freedom of conscience stems from the dialectical-materialistic concept of the nature of religion and its essence as a distorted form of social conscience, which arises and develops on the basis of the social and political conditions of life. While, at the earlier stages of mankind's development these conditions consisted in the full dependence of people on the elements and the feeling of helplessness and awe before them, with the division of society into classes the religious world outlook came to be based, as Lenin pointed out, on "the socially downtrodden condition of the working masses and their apparently complete helplessness in the face of the blind forces of capitalism, which every day and every hour inflict upon ordinary working people the most horrible suffering and the most savage torment, a thousand times more severe than those inflicted by extraordinary events, such as wars, earthquakes, etc."[2]

In a society rent by class antagonisms, religious views serve as a kind of protest on the part of the believers against the exploitative system, against their political and socioeconomic oppression. "Religion," Marx said, "is the sigh of the oppressed

[1] V.I.Lenin, *Collected Works*, Vol. 10, p. 84.
[2] V.I. Lenin, *Collected Works*, Vol. 15, pp. 405–406.

creature, the heart of a heartless world . . . It is the *opium* of the people."[1]

The exploiting classes are interested in religion as an instrument of perpetuating their dominance over the masses. They prevent in every way the dissemination of correct, scientific views on nature and society among the working people, considering, not without foundation, that people who are ignorant and believe in God are more easily subjegated and oppressed. An example of this is the position of religion in our country prior to the Great October Socialist Revolution.

In czarist Russia, the church was a state institution. It was the duty of every subject of the Russian Empire to profess some faith. Dissemination of materialist views and antireligious propaganda were prohibited.

The state legislatively interfered in the internal affairs of religious associations. The priests' status was virtually that of officials. There were special state-run schools (seminaries) where Orthodox clergymen were trained. By the beginning of this century Russia had almost 69,000 Orthodox churches, 110,000 priests and 58,000 monks. By way of comparison, it may be noted that in 1913 the total number of scientific workers, physicians and teachers in the country was only about 320,000.

The alliance of the church and the state rested on a firm economic basis. The clergy were paid large subsidies, salaries and various allowances. For instance, in 1907, the Holy Synod was allocated 29 million rubles, almost as much as was allocated for the Ministry of Public Education. The church owned immense property, including tracts of land, trading enterprises and bank accounts.

Being part of the machinery of state, the church exerted an exceedingly strong influence on the social and private lives of people. Birth, marriage and death certificates were issued by the church authorities. A marriage contracted without the sanction of the church was regarded as unlawful and the children born of such a marriage were considered "illegitimate." Those who did

[1]Karl Marx and Frederick Engels, *Collected Works*, Vol. 3, p. 175.

not abide by the precepts of religion were threatened with dismissal from work. For instance, the great Russian scientist Klimenty Timiryazev was dismissed for "godlessness" from the Agricultural Academy, which bears his name today.

Almost half of the country's schools were in the hands of the church. The Orthodox faith was an obligatory subject in all schools, both state-financed and private, and it was the principal subject in the primary and parish schools. School authorities saw to it that the pupils attended church services and performed religious rites. Religion was forcibly imposed also on institutions of higher learning.

It must be said that under czarism not only "godless" people were discriminated against, but also people who professed faiths other than the Orthodox one. There were many religions in Russia (Catholic, Protestant, Islam, Judaism, Buddhist, etc.), but Orthodoxy was pre-eminent. The Orthodox Church enjoyed the protection and support of the state, and the czar was regarded as its head.

Only members of the Orthodox Church could hold government posts. The laws of the empire were such that those who rejected Orthodoxy were held to oppose the czar and were subject to deprivation of all rights and internal exile. Conversion from the Orthodox faith to any other faith was allowed only in exceptional cases. Followers of certain religions were restricted in their right to choose a place of residence. Few people belonging to any other religion were admitted to educational institutions. The laws of the empire forbade mixed marriages, thus fomenting national-religious strife between the peoples.

Obviously, with the enforcement of such medieval inquisitorial laws persecuting people on grounds of faith or atheism, there could be no question of freedom of conscience in Russia.

The position of the Communist Party in the sphere of religion was formulated in its First program. It called for unrestricted freedom of conscience, complete equality of citizens irrespective of religion, and separation of the church from the state and the school. The implementation of these principles became possible after the Great October Socialist Revolution.

The principle of freedom of conscience was fully embodied in

Soviet legislation. The decree drafted by Lenin and issued on January 20, 1918, "On the Separation of the Church from the State and of the School from the Church" established the right of every citizen to profess any faith or none at all, eliminated any liability connected with professing or not professing any religion and proclaimed the equality of all religions before the law.

The decree not only proclaimed freedom of conscience, but also secured it by separating the church from the state and the school from the church. The separation of the church from the state meant that state agencies were not to interfere in the internal affairs of religious associations and that the church was not to interfere in the affairs of the state and in the activities of political and economic organizations and of health-protection, educational, social security and other agencies. All civic registration functions (registration of marriage, birth, etc.) were transferred from the church to Soviet agencies.

All ecclesiastical and religious associations were deprived of the support and financial assistance of the state. They were to observe the general statutes and rules concerning private societies and associations, and their land and other property were nationalized. The decree forbade them from applying measures of compulsion and punishment to believers or from forcibly extracting any duties or taxes.

The separation of the school from the church meant that the church would not be permitted to teach religion in schools, force students to study religion or interfere in the education of the younger generation.

At the same time, the decree "On the Separation of the Church from the State and the School from the Church" ensured for believers the right to freely perform religious rites "in so far as they do not violate public order and are not accompanied by encroachments on the rights of citizens of the Soviet Republic."

Thus, the Soviet state legislatively put an end to the violence committed against the conscience of citizens by both government agencies and the church. The basic principles of Lenin's decree were embodied in Soviet legislation on religious worship and written into all Soviet constitutions, including the 1977 Constitution.

As was to be expected, the clergy, which had been one of the pillars of the monarchy and was now deprived of its privileges, vehemently attacked the revolutionary laws on religion and the church and offered fierce resistance to Soviet power. "Regiments of Jesus", "Regiments of the Holy Virgin" and "Holy Cross detachments" were formed in the years of the Civil War, when foreign military forces intervened to fight against the Red Army. Monasteries often served as bases for the counterrevolution. In fact, not a single counterrevolutionary uprising took place without the complicity or even direct participation of clergymen.

It is natural, therefore, that the struggle against the enemies of the socialist state included also the struggle against those reactionary clerics who engaged in activities hostile to the Soviet people. However, many members of the clergy realized that its opposition to Soviet power was undermining the authority of the church and its influence among the masses. Of great importance in this connection was the Party's policy toward religion. Even in the most difficult moments of the Civil War and foreign intervention the principle of freedom of conscience was strictly observed.

As socialist construction got under way and the Soviet state was consolidated, the clergy was faced with a dilemma: It had either to recognize Soviet power unconditionally or lose all believers' support. Already in 1923, representatives of an influential religious trend which called for "renovation" of the Orthodox Church on the principles of recognizing the new Soviet power, addressed a message of greetings to the Soviet Government, which said in part: "Using state methods, the Great October Revolution . . . is carrying out the great principles of equality and labor . . . All over the world the strong oppress the weak. Only in Soviet Russia has the struggle against this injustice begun. The Council believes that every upright citizen should take an active stand among these fighters for human truth, implementing in every way the principles of the

October Revolution." In subsequent years, under the pressure of believers, the heads of the majority of religious faiths declared their loyalty to Soviet power.

The victory of the socialist revolution opened up broad possibilities for the propagation of materialist views, for conducting scientific enlightenment work among the masses, and this work yielded results. Already in the mid-thirties, two-thirds of the adult population in the cities and one-third in the countryside were nonbelievers. Since then, atheistic convictions have become much more widespread. Sociological surveys conducted in a number of regions, cities and districts show that active believers (those who more or less regularly keep Lent, go to confession, attend church services, etc.) account for about 8–10 percent of the adult population. Atheists make up 97–98 percent of young people aged under 20. The church has lost its influence on the most socially active sections of the population: skilled workers and the intelligentsia.

To our Party, the struggle against religious prejudices has always been an ideological struggle of a scientific, materialist world view against an antiscientific, religious one. We are waging this struggle only by means of persuasion and education. The Communist Party has always held that all attempts to make believers give up their convictions by coercive measures are not only futile, but also harmful, that atheism can be spread, not through prohibiting religion, but by means of consistent persuasion, by drawing believers into an active social life. After all, you can't order a man to think scientifically.

The Party repeatedly stressed in its decisions how important it is to avoid offending the feelings of believers, for this could only strengthen religious fanaticism. It firmly put a stop to instances of administrative interference in the activities of religious associations and groups, rudeness to the clergy and offensive attacks on believers attending religious services. In 1954, the CPSU Central Committee adopted a resolution "On Mistakes in the Conduct of Scientific Atheistic Propaganda Among the Population," in which it pointed to the need "to bear in mind that offensive acts against the church, the clergy and believing citizens are incompatible with the line of the Party and the state in the conduct of scientific atheistic propaganda and contradict the Constitution of the USSR, which grants freedom of conscience to Soviet citizens.

Defending the rights of believers, an attitude of trust by the Soviet state to the church, is one of the principles of socialist law. *The USSR Constitution guarantees to Soviet citizens the right to profess any religion and to conduct religious worship, and prohibits incitement of hostility or hatred on religious grounds.* Soviet legislation has established special regulations to prevent encroachments on the legitimate rights of believers, religious associations, and churchgoers. Provisions have been made for punishing any interference with religious worship if it is conducted within the framework of Soviet laws. No special permission from the authorities is needed for religious processions around churches which are part of the service unless they obstruct traffic.

Any discrimination against believers is prohibited. Refusal to employ a person or to admit him to an educational establishment, dismissal from work or an educational institution, deprivation of legitimate privileges or any other limitation of a person's rights on religious grounds are punishable by law. Soviet legislation does not prohibit religious instruction of children. It can be conducted privately, that is, in the family, by the parents. Children can go to church and attend services. Citizens who have reached the age of 18 have the right to join religious associations and groups.

Our laws prohibit closing churches and prayer houses if they are supported by the population. More than 20,000 Orthodox, Catholic, Lutheran and Old Believers' churches, synagogues, mosques, Buddhist lamaseries, prayer houses of the Evangelical Christians, Baptists and Seventh Day Adventists, as well as 19 monasteries and convents are functioning freely in the USSR. Under the law, all church premises and prayer houses are the property of the whole people (the state) and are made available for free use to believers united in religious associations.

Among the church buildings there are hundreds of architectural monuments, remarkable creations of the people's genius. The outstanding works of architecture and art are under the protection of the state, which allocates considerable funds for repair and restoration work. The churches have their own facilities for making articles used in religious worship, with the necessary raw materials and other supplies provided by the state on a planned basis. All religious associations have the right to acquire transportation and to erect, buy or rent buildings for their needs. The funds of the church, consisting of the voluntary offerings of believers and proceeds from the sale of religious objects, are not taxable.

The religious centers regularly put out their publications: the Bible, the Koran, theological works, prayer books, journals, church calendars—up to 50 different books regularly. Besides, some of them receive periodicals from their fellow worshipers abroad.

Religious associations have the right to train their clergy. There are 18 higher and secondary religious schools, among them six Orthodox academies and seminaries, a Moslem academy and a madrasah; an academy of the Armenian Church, a seminary of the Georgian Orthodox Church, etc., which have all the facilities necessary for their work. For instance, the library of the Leningrad Orthodox Theological Academy has about 200,000 volumes of theological works in many languages. The organization of the teaching process and internal rules in the theological schools are the prerogative of the religious bodies themselves.

Believers can hold meetings and conferences and elect their leading bodies to decide matters pertaining to the management of the affairs, property and funds of the religious associations, and pertaining to external relations. The religious centers and boards are absolutely autonomous in dealing with all matters of church life. They maintain contacts and correspondence with religious associations in other countries, send representatives to their conventions and conferences and take an active part in the work of international religious organizations. Every year more than 10 delegations of religious associations go abroad and approximately as many foreign religious delegations visit the Soviet Union.

While granting and protecting the rights of believers and the church, the USSR Constitution stresses the duty of all Soviet citizens, believers included, to observe the country's laws and regulations. It is forbidden in the Soviet Union to organize religious groups whose rites do harm to the health of citizens or those which incite citizens to neglect their civic duties.

It must be said that the majority of the clergy honestly comply with Soviet laws. At times, however, some church or near-church extremists try to contravene them, mostly for selfish ends. Quite understandably, they are called to account and sometimes brought before a court of law.

The Council for Religious Affairs, which is a Soviet government body, sees to the observance of all the laws pertaining to the activities of religious associations, without interfering in their internal affairs.

The attitude of the Communist Party and the Soviet state to religion and the church is often misrepresented in the West. Stories are spread about persecution of the clergy and believers about infringement on the freedom of conscience by Soviet legislation on religious worship, about suppression of religion by violent methods in our country, about there being "compulsory atheism" in the USSR. The groundlessness of these allegations is evident to all who are familiar with the actual position of believers and the church in the Soviet Union. This is acknowledged by church dignitaries in the Soviet Union, and this is seen by numerous visitors from abroad.

It has become customary for Western propaganda, noted the editor-in-chief of the journal, *Islam and the Modern World,* A.B.M. Shamsuddoulah, to assert that Moslems are repressed in the USSR. Regrettably, some people believe in such cock-and-bull stories. If one, for example, will visit Tajikistan, they will see that the life of Moslems is good there, that they enjoy all the benefits of civilization and education and do not suffer from unemployment. The USSR is not a Moslem country, but the government of the Soviet Union has granted to Moslems rights and opportunities that have never been granted in the Moslem countries.

In the past few years the religious organizations in our country have reaffirmed, at major forums, their sincere support for the Soviet social and state system and for the USSR Constitution, and their approval of the internal and foreign policy of the

Communist Party and the Soviet state. Together with all the Soviet people, they come out for peace, for friendship among all nations. Representatives of almost all religions from 107 countries attended the world conference "Religious Workers for Lasting Peace, Disarmament and Just Relations among Nations," which was held in the USSR in 1977. In 1979, in Dushanbe, the capital of Soviet Tajikistan, a symposium was held on "The Contribution of the Moslems of Central Asia, the Volga Region and the Caucasus to the Development of Islamic Thought, to the Cause of Peace and Social Progress," in which church dignitaries from Soviet republics and prominent representatives of the Moslem clergy from 25 countries took part.

II. RIGHTS AND FREEDOMS

THE SOCIOECONOMIC SPHERE

The socioeconomic rights of Soviet citizens enshrined in the USSR Constitution include the right to work, rest and recreation, health protection, social maintenance and housing. The country's well-developed economy, which is the property of the whole people, is a reliable material guarantee of these rights. The Soviet economy is developing in accordance with a single plan which outlines concrete social aims. The socialist system of economy ensures crisis-free, stable and dynamic development of all its branches, the growth of public wealth and improvement of the living standards of the people.

When setting social aims we naturally proceed from the real possibilities of the economy, for only that can be consumed which has been produced. But our attitude to what is possible and what is not possible depends, in turn, on the social aims. It is known, for instance, that the United States still exceeds us in the national income produced. But, for all its wealth, the United States is unavoidably burdened with a vast army of unemployed, while there is no unemployment in our country. Thus, what matters is not only the level of production as such, but also the kind of problems the produced wealth is used to solve.

The Soviet state began its economic activity in conditions not merely of poverty, but of economic devastation, of the decline of all branches of the economy and an acute shortage of skilled workers and specialists. The nationalization of industry and the banks made it possible to concentrate resources on solving problems in what we regarded as decisive sectors, and to pursue an investment policy geared to the stupendous tasks we had set for ourselves.

The key task was formulated by the Communist Party when it became the ruling party. It was industrialization, establishing a highly efficient machine-building industry based on the achievements of science and technology.

A vital prerequisite for this was the implementation of the State Plan for the Electrification of Russia, known as the GOELRO Plan, the world's first nationwide plan for economic development, worked out on Lenin's initiative. With this plan the history of a scientifically-based, comprehensive and planned approach to running the economy began.

Using the advantages of centralized planning, the Party solved the cardinal problems of industrialization in a historically short space of time. A material base was laid for strengthening the economic independence of the USSR, for the retooling of all the branches of the national economy and for the collectivization of agriculture. Industrialization consolidated public ownership in the decisive sphere of the economy, made possible the ousting of capitalist elements and the establishment of the socialist system in industry, ensured the growth of the working class and its leading role in society, strengthened the economic and defense capacity of the USSR and, in many respects, predetermined our victory in the Great Patriotic War against nazi Germany.

The victory cost us dearly; rehabilitation of the economy required great expenditure of material and financial resources, and this could not help but affect any improvement of the people's well-being. Only comparatively recently, in the latter half of the 1960s, did a sharper turn to raising the standard of living become apparent.

The socioeconomic program of the last three congresses of the CPSU (the 24th, 25th and 26th) are programs in which the fuller satisfaction of the material and intellectual requirements of people is set as the principal objective. About three-quarters of the national income produced in 1980, or approximately four-fifths if the expenditure on housing construction and on social and cultural needs is included, was used for consumption. Today the Soviet Union's social product is 130 percent larger than in 1965, to say nothing of before. For instance, in 1980 the national income was 75 times greater than before the revolution.

The 26th Congress of the CPSU put forward an extensive program of further improving the people's well-being in the 11th Five-Year Plan period and throughout the 1980s. This program envisages an improvement in all aspects of the lives of Soviet people—consumption and housing, culture and recreation, working conditions and services offered.

As socialist production develops, its efficiency rises, the quality of work in all branches of the national economy improves, the socioeconomic needs of citizens are better fulfilled and the guarantees of these needs being fulfilled become ever more reliable.

A BASIC HUMAN RIGHT

> Citizens of the USSR have the
> right to work . . . From Article 40
> of the USSR Constitution

To Soviet people, the right to work is something that goes without saying. Unemployment was done away with in the USSR half a century ago.

But during the transition from capitalism to socialism, unemployment was a major social problem in the USSR, whose solution demanded considerable efforts and the overcoming of innumerable obstacles.

Mass chronic unemployment appeared in the world with the development of capitalism. The emergence of an "industrial reserve army" was explained by the founders of scientific communism. They proved that the existence of an army of unemployed enabled entrepreneurs to intensify the exploitation of the proletariat. "The over-work of the employed part of the working class," Marx pointed out, "swells the ranks of the reserve, whilst conversely the greater pressure that the latter by its competition exerts on the former, forces these to submit to over-work and to subjugation under the dictates of capital."[1]

The scientific conclusions of Marx and Engels on the "surplus population" and the "industrial reserve army" born of the capitalist system were elaborated by Lenin, who proved that it is impossible to solve the problem of unemployment under capitalism,[2] and that its only solution lies in the class struggle of the proletariat.[3]

Nationalization of large-scale industry and of land, the introduction of Workers' Control, and the introduction of an 8-hour working day were material prerequisites for doing away with unemployment and its causes. Immediately after the establishment of Soviet power a People's Commissariat (ministry) for Labor was set up, whose functions included keeping stock of and distributing labor resources, drafting legislative acts on labor and organizing relief to the unemployed. The first Soviet Labor Code proclaimed the right of all citizens to work according to their qualifications.

However, the Soviet state could not immediately provide jobs to all because of the huge reserve army of labor inherited from old Russia. Besides, the ranks of the unemployed were swelled as the Russian army was demobilized and munitions manufacture was curtailed following the withdrawal of Soviet Russia from the imperialist war.

An aggravating factor here was that the implementation of Soviet government decrees in the sphere of labor was fiercely

[1]Karl Marx, *Capital,* Vol. 1, Progress Publishers, Moscow, p. 595.
[2]See V.I. Lenin, *Collected Works,* Vol. 11, p. 304.
[3]Ibid., Vol. 5, p. 278.

resisted, especially at the outset, by the entrepreneurs, who still retained some positions in the economy. Referring to the lack of fuel, factory owners often closed down enterprises, conducted unannounced lock outs and kept secret "black lists" of workers.

The petty bourgeois parties of Socialist Revolutionaries and Mensheviks attempted to take advantage of unemployment and hunger. They put the blame for unemployment on the Communist Party and Soviet government and sought to rouse the working people to counterrevolutionary actions and strikes.

The country's industry, which was undergoing a deep crisis as a result of the imperialist war, economic breakdown and the sabotage and lock-outs carried out by entrepreneurs, could not absorb the huge mass of jobless people. It became an urgent task to organize relief for them.

"Regulations on Insurance in the Event of Unemployment" were adopted. They were valid throughout the country and applied to all persons employed in state and private enterprises, institutions and public organizations. All insurance payments were made by entrepreneurs, and on the basis of these contributions an All-Russia Unemployment Fund was set up. Unemployment allowances were paid through insurance offices staffed by representatives of workers' organizations. Despite an acute shortage of funds, canteens and hostels for the particularly needy unemployed were organized in many cities.

In early 1918, Soviet government bodies began to establish a network of labor exchanges. Eventually these became authoritative organizations in charge of the registration and distribution of the labor force.

The principal measure in combating unemployment was, of course, rehabilitation of the ruined economy and its restructuring on socialist principles. But peaceful construction was disrupted in the summer of 1918 by the armed intervention of imperialist powers supported by internal counterrevolution.

Hundreds of thousands of workers joined the ranks of the Soviet Army in response to a call from the Communist Party. Acute food shortages in the cities drove a part of the unemployment disappeared in the cities. By the end of 1918, the labor exchanges were already having difficulties in meeting the requests of enterprises; the demand for labor considerably exceeded the supply. Instead of unemployment a new problem, a shortage of labor, arose.

However, the root causes of unemployment were not yet eliminated. The Party was well aware that a strenuous struggle lay ahead against overpopulation in the countryside, the declassing of the working class and other adverse phenomena. In view of this, its Second Program set as a top-priority task "maximum utilization of all the available labor force in the state, its correct distribution and redistribution both between different regions and between different branches of the national economy." The Party also considered it necessary "to return to working life all who have been sidetracked from it."

After the Civil War and foreign intervention there was a new wave of unemployment, which added to the many difficulties facing the country. In January 1922, 160,000 unemployed were registered at the labor exchanges. A year later the figure rose to 641,000 and by July 1924, to more than 1,344,000. The 15th Party Congress in 1927 described unemployment as one of the greatest difficulties the country faced in carrying out socialist construction.

As the rehabilitation of the national economy proceeded and the life of the urban population began to improve, the influx of rural residents into the cities again increased. "For some categories of workers (unskilled workers, domestic servants, poorly qualified office staff, etc.)," it was noted in a resolution of the 15th Conference of the Party, "unemployment threatens to become chronic in the nearest future, owing to overpopulation in the countryside and the constant influx of labor from the countryside into the cities."

Unemployment was also due to the immense damage done to the national economy during the Civil War. In 1921, gross industrial output was one-third of the 1917 volume, while the number of workers had fallen from 2,596,000 to 1,185,000. The ranks of the unemployed were further augmented following the demobilization of the army.

The Party took a number of measures to deal with the situation, including registration and job placement through labor exchanges, the large-scale development of public works (removal of construction debris in the cities, draining bogs, filling in ravines, etc.) and organization of the unemployed into work collectives, which not only provided them with jobs but also taught them trades.

It should be stressed, however, that the Communist Party saw its main task not in easing the plight of the unemployed and reducing unemployment, but in abolishing unemployment altogether.

The industrialization of the country and the collectivization of agriculture marked the decisive stage in the fight against unemployment. Lenin's plan for building socialism was, at the same time, a plan for eliminating unemployment in the USSR.

By 1926 the rehabilitation of the national economy was almost completed. Our country entered a new period of development —a period of socialist reconstruction on the basis of industrialization. The 14th Party Congress (December 1925) mapped out a course for the rapid development of heavy industry, which could equip other industries and agriculture with the latest technology, turning the USSR from an agrarian into an industrial country and ensuring the construction of a socialist society. The Party regarded the development of industry as the decisive condition for increasing the ranks of the working class and thus for eliminating unemployment.

Special attention was paid to the coal, oil, electrical engineering, automotive, tractor, defense and some other industries. The construction of new railroad lines was extended. Local craft industries were also developed.

The rapid construction of industrial enterprises led to a considerable decline in the number of unemployed skilled workers. However, at the end of 1926, there were still 1,310,000 registered unemployed, many of whom lacked the skills required by the national economy.

The Party Central Committee adopted a resolution on the training of skilled workers which would include—and this was particularly emphasized—the unemployed.

Special attention was given to training unemployed juveniles, whose number, whose number, registered at the labor exchanges in October 1925, was more than 122,000. By a government decision the network of factory schools was expanded. By 1929 the number of jeveniles attending these schools had reached 163,000.

When speaking of the solution of the problem of unemployment in the Soviet Union, mention must be made of the cultural-enlightenment work conducted among the unemployed. Wherever large numbers of unemployed were found —at labor exchanges, in boarding houses, tea houses, canteens —reading rooms and libraries were organized, as well as courses for teaching people to read and write, for giving them further training, etc. It was explained to the unemployed that much depended on them themselves, that they should not lose heart but actively prepare for the time when there would be jobs for everybody.

In the final battle against unemployment the decisive role was played by the first five-year plan (1929–32) for the country's socioeconomic development. It was a period of rapid construction of new industrial projects, the commissioning of giant industrial enterprises and growth in the ranks of the working class. An intensive process of socialist construction was under way in the countryside. The Party's course for the collectivization of agriculture, charted at its 15th Congress, was, at the same time, aimed at eliminating the main source of unemployment —overpopulation in the countryside.

Unemployment declined rapidly as industry developed and the influx of unemployed manpower from the countryside into the cities stopped. In December 1929, the Central Committee of the Party adopted a resolution "On the Growth of Working-Class Cadres, the State of Unemployment, and Measures to Reduce It." The resolution called for better planning of the training and distribution of manpower and the training and distribution of the unemployed. Economic agencies were instructed to assess as quickly as possible the demand for skilled labor and to work out a system of measures guaranteeing the timely and sufficient supply of skilled labor to industry, transport and agriculture. Additional funds were allocated for these purposes and also for the expansion of the factory school–training system.

In early 1930, a careful check of labor exchanges in the majority of cities showed that the recipients of unemployment benefits included many persons who simply did not want to work: vagrants, petty thieves, speculators, etc. After a purge at the Moscow labor exchange, one of the country's biggest, only 177 unemployed remained on the list.

In the autumn of the same year about 300,000 young people were enrolled in factory schools; this put an end to juvenile unemployment. On October 9, 1930, the People's Commissariat for Labor adopted a decision on the immediate provision of jobs to all the remaining unemployed and the abolition of unemployment benefits.

Thus, by the end of 1930, unemployment had been virtually eliminated in the USSR. The 17th Party Congress (1934) noted: "Having overcome tremendous difficulties arising from the implementation of the five-year plan, the proletariat has scored historic victories in improving the condition of the working people of town and country . . . The worker and the collective farmer are now fully confident of the morrow, and the continuous rise of their material and cultural levels depends only on the quality and quantity of their work. The working man in the USSR is no longer threatened with unemployment, poverty and hunger."

The right to work had become a real right in the USSR. It was written down in the 1936 Constitution of the USSR as a major gain of socialism.

As on many previous occasions, Western propaganda hastened to declare that the absence of unemployment in the USSR was temporary, and that as soon as it embarked upon the path of technical progress, the USSR would again be faced with this problem. Historical experience has refuted this prophecy.

Now, why is there no unemployment in the USSR? Why is unemployment impossible in our country?

In the first place, political power in our country belongs to the whole people, who are the masters of the instruments and means of production. An end has thus been put to a situation whereby the number of jobs was determined by entrepreneurs who were guided only by their personal interests.

In addition, the socialist economy is planned. It can achieve accelerated technical progress while, at the same time, ensuring full employment of the able-bodied population. "We have the means for determining in advance not only the volume of production needed, but also the requisite size and professional composition of the work force. In other words, production plans are drawn up on the basis of available labor resources, guaranteeing employment to all who can work. This concerns also young people graduating from vocational, specialized secondary and higher schools.

Increased efficiency of production does not result in redundancy. The planned character of the economy makes it possible to set such rates of development in industry that demand for labor has, for half a century now, exceeded supply. For instance, in the 10th Five-Year Plan period (1975–1980) alone, more than 1,200 large industrial enterprises went into operation in our country.

In contrast to this, unemployment in the developed capitalist countries has reached an unprecedented level in the past 40 years and continues to grow. The number of officially registered unemployed in these countries was 8 million in 1970, more than 15 million in 1975 and about 20 million in 1980. In the past 10 years official data shows that the number of jobless in the United States went up from 4 million to 8.5 million, which is almost 8 percent of the able-bodied population. And this is not complete data. Figures released by trade unions centers show that in early 1980 there were more than 25 million jobless people in 11 major capitalist countries, including close to 12 million in the United States.

Until recently the growth of the number of wage-earning and salaried workers employed in the USSR's national economy was exceedingly rapid: 11.4 million in 1928, 33.9 million in 1940, 76.9 million in 1965 and 112.5 million in 1980. But in the 1980s the rates of this growth will decrease and the problem of labor resources will become more acute as the consequences of the

Great Patriotic War, in which the country lost 20 million people, will begin to be felt. Hence the need, as was pointed out at the 25th and 26th Party congresses, for a sharp increase in productivity and efficiency in social production.

The Soviet Constitution guarantees the right to work and pay in accordance with the quantity and quality of work, and not below the state-established minimum. Today, in nearly 50 percent of the families in the country, there is a monthly income of more than 100 rubles per member of the family, as against only 4 percent in 1965. Differences in living standards between different social groups have been steadily diminishing.

It was decided at the 26th Congress of the CPSU to begin implementation of an important social measure—to raise the minimal monthly wage or salary to 80 rubles. It is planned to increase the average monthly wages and salaries to 190–195 rubles by 1985. The incomes of collective farmers will grow by 20–22 percent. Provision is also being made for extending of wage benefits.

The constitutional right to work includes *the right to choose a trade or profession, type of job and work in accordance with one's inclinations, abilities, training and education.* Of course, this does not mean that everything depends on a person's wishes, that he is not to exert any efforts, that his choice is not in any way influenced by objective circumstances and the requirements of society. Social requirements manifest themselves in the fact that the number of educational establishments providing training in different specializations varies, that, for instance, it is easier to enroll in a building college than in the biology department of a university, and so on.

The growth of the productive forces and scientific and technical progress give rise to the demand for personnel with new skills and higher qualifications. Thus, to ensure the right to work, *our state provides free vocational training, organizes programs for improvement of skills and training in new trades and professions, and develops the system of vocational guidance and job placement.* These provisions, too, are to be found in the 1977 Constitution.

Soviet society is a society of working people. As was noted at the 26th Congress, the Party and the state have been and are doing much to make the work of people not only more productive, but also more meaningful, interesting and creative.

Thus, it has been proved in practice that only under socialism is it possible to do away completely with unemployment and to ensure the right to work. Full employment under socialism, unemployment under capitalism—such are characteristic features of the two social systems. The sympathies of Soviet people are with the working people in the capitalist countries, and they support them in their just struggle for this basic human right, the right to work.

ONE OF THE MOST IMPORTANT TASKS

> Citizens of the USSR have the right to rest and leisure. From Article 41 of the USSR Constitution.
>
> Citizens of the USSR have the right to health protection. From Article 42 of the USSR Constitution.

Today, when Soviet people enjoy the right to rest and leisure as a matter of course, when the successes of the Soviet health-protection system are known the world over, it may be useful to recall what the conditions of work, rest and leisure and health protection for working people were in prerevolutionary Russia.

People worked 12–13 hours a day in factories and plants and 15–16 hours in the textile industry. One day of rest on Sunday was insufficient to restore one's strength after a week of exhausting work, and the workers had no annual vacations.

The peasants were even worse off. Farmhands slaved for landlords and kulaks from dawn to dusk. The following clauses were written in the contract which women applying for work on the estate of Count Potocki had to sign in 1905: "I, a peasant woman of . . . village, have become employed of my own free will at . . . farm belonging to Count Potocki, to do whatever farm work I may be told to do . . . I pledge myself to work from sunrise to sunset . . . I have no right to refuse if the estate summons me to work on a holiday or Sunday . . . if I fall sick or die, my family shall do my work. . . . These conditions are known to me, which I attest with my signature."

There was no labor protection in factories and mines. In 1902 Batumi workers wrote to the newspaper *Iskra:* ". . . Workers in soldering shops of oil refineries suffer from throat and chest diseases, for the air in these shops is saturated with the vapors of acids. In the pouring shops of these refineries workers' legs are swollen and covered with sores from kerosene . . . It's hard to find a worker there who is not afflicted with fever and rheumatism." Accidents, cave-ins, explosions and flooding in mines were common.

The czarist government did practically nothing in the sphere of public health. In 1913, there was one hospital bed per 767 people and one doctor for 5,656 people. As for treatment at sanatoriums, landowners, members of the nobility and rich merchants were 42 percent of those spending holidays and taking treatment at the Caucasian spas in 1907; factory owners and rich farmers—24 percent; government officials and army officers—23 percent; scientists and doctors—10 percent, and clergymen—1 percent.

Periodic epidemics of typhus, cholera, the plague and smallpox spread over whole regions and took hundreds of thousands of lives. Every year about three percent of the population died in czarist Russia for lack of medical care. Before the First World War mortality was almost twice higher and child mortality, three to four times higher than in England, Germany, Norway, the United States and France.

Our Party always regarded it as one of its principal social tasks to struggle for a shorter working day, for the right of working people to rest and leisure and to health protection. In its First Program, "in the interests of the protection of the working class from physical and moral degeneration, as well as in the interests of the development of its capacity for liberation struggle," the Party called for limitation of the working day to eight hours for all wage workers; establishment by law of a weekly rest lasting, continuously, at least 42 hours; complete prohibition of overtime; prohibition of night shifts, with the exception of industries where they were absolutely necessary; prohibition of the use by entrepreneurs of the labor of children of school age (up to 16 years), limitation of the working time of juveniles (16–18 years) to six hours; and prohibition of female labor where it was harmful to women's health.

The Party's program also called for the properly organized sanitary inspection at all enterprises employing wage labor; the establishment of criminal liability for entrepreneurs who violated labor protection laws; free medical assistance to workers to be financed by the entrepreneurs, with workers getting paid for the period of illness; and inspection by the local authorities of the sanitary conditions of the houses allotted to workers by the entrepreneurs.

All this was achieved in Russia only through revolutionary struggle. On the eve of the Great October Socialist Revolution, the majority of the workers, juveniles included, worked for 10 hours a day, and about 15 percent of them, for 11, 12 or more hours. "The dialectics of the class struggle are such," Lenin pointed out, "that, unless there is an extreme need, unless it is the last remedy, the bourgeoisie will never replace the tranquil, habitual, profitable . . . ten-hour day by an eight-hour one."[1]

The socialist revolution was this "extreme need." Three days after its victory, the Council of People's Commissars adopted a decree introducing an eight-hour day. The Soviet government enacted legislation on all the points outlined in the Party's First Program in the sphere of labor protection and incorporated them in a Code of Labor Laws.

In its Second Program the Communist Party committed itself

[1]V.I. Lenin, *Collected Works*, Vol. 18, p. 293.

to subsequently introducing, given an overall increase in labor productivity, a still shorter working day without reducing pay.

On October 15, 1927, on the 10th anniversary of the October Revolution, the Soviet Government adopted a manifesto proclaiming the transition from an eight hour working day to a seven-hour day, with no cuts in pay. In the next five to six years a seven-hour day was introduced for the majority of wage-earning and salaried workers, but the threat of aggression posed by Nazi Germany compelled us to restore the eight-hour day, and soon after the war broke out the managers of enterprises were given the right to establish, with the permission of the government, obligatory overtime amounting to one to three hours daily. Regular annual and additional leaves were cancelled. That was understandable to all, war is war.

After the victory, the prewar conditions of labor and rest and leisure for wage-earning and salaried workers were restored: Obligatory overtime was abolished, and annual holidays were reintroduced. However, in view of the vast destruction inflicted on the national economy, an eight-hour day for most workers, with the exception of those working in arduous conditions, had to be retained.

After the completion of postwar rehabilitation and the successful implementation of economic development plans, the Communist Party again put forward the task of reducing the working day. In 1956, a decision was adopted on going over everywhere to a seven- and six-hour day. From 1966, there began the systematic transfer of wage-earning and salaried workers to a five-day working week. The changeover was largely completed by the 50th anniversary of the October Revolution. As a result, we now have 112 days off a year, including holidays, instead of 60 under the six-day working week.

Reduction of the length of the working day is one of the most important guarantees of the right of Soviet people to rest and leisure. *In accordance with the USSR Constitution the working week for wage and salary workers does not exceed 41 hours, and it is shorter for a number of trades and professions and industries, shorter hours for night work have been established, and all working people are provided with weekly days of rest and paid annual holidays.*

The working week in the USSR is one of the shortest in the world. Over the years of Soviet government the length of the working week in industry has been cut by almost one-third.

As we see it, leisure time is a yardstick of public wealth. Today people use it not so much for rest as for the satisfaction of a wide range of intellectual needs such as studying, participating in social activity, raising children, reading, playing sports, traveling, pursuing hobbies, going to see movies, going to museums, theaters, etc. Thus, in keeping with the Constitution, the state ensures the right to rest and leisure *by extending the network of cultural, educational and health-building institutions; developing, on a mass scale, sports, physical culture, camping and tourism; providing more opportunities for the rational use of free time.*

Priority is given, of course, to measures that directly or indirectly help strengthen the health of people. In May 1921 the government issued a decree on the organization of a broad network of holiday homes for workers. Country houses, former landowners' estates, former monasteries, etc., were used for this purpose at first. Even in the years when the young Soviet state was short of funds for building vital economic projects, old holiday homes and sanatoria were restored and renovated and new ones were built.

In subsequent years expenditures for these aims grew steadily. Between 1939 and 1980, the number of sanatoria and recreational institutions rose from 3,600 to 13,160, and the number of their guests, from 469,000 to more than two million. In the past 10 years the number of people who stayed in sanatoria, holiday homes (excluding short, one- or two-day holidays) and at tourist centers grew by 130 percent, reaching 39 million in 1980. Eighty-six percent of the vouchers for sanatoria, rest homes, holiday homes and after-work sanatoria were issued at reduced cost, with the difference being covered by social maintenance funds, and 17 percent of the vouchers were issued free of charge.

Extensive facilities have been provided for sports and physical culture. They include about 200 sports palaces and indoor stadiums, more than 3,500 open-air stadiums, 110,000 football fields, 74,000 gymnasiums, 6,300 skiing centers, 8,500 track and field stadiums and 1,700 swimming pools. About 318,000 full-time workers are employed in the physical culture movement. Sports and physical culture specialists are trained at more than 220 higher and specialized secondary schools.

More than 70 sports are actively cultivated in the USSR. Every year there are up to 500 countrywide sports competitions, and once every four years the USSR Peoples' Games (called Spartakiads) are held. About 100 million people took part in the 7th Spartakiad in 1979.

The broad scope of the physical culture movement accounts for the successes of Soviet athletes in international sports. The 22nd Olympics in Moscow are convincing evidence of this.

A major achievement of socialism is the unified state-run health-protection system ensuring free qualified medical assistance to all citizens.

The first step in building this system was the nationalization of medical institutions and enterprises. All medical and health-building institutions, pharmacies, health resorts, etc., were placed under the People's Commissariat for Health Protection, which was formed in July 1918. In the first 18 months after the revolution, Lenin signed about 300 government documents bearing on questions of public health protection.

Those were extremely difficult years. The Civil War was raging. Industrial and agricultural production had dropped sharply. The population was famished. At the end of 1918 the daily ration of bread, even for first-category workers, was a mere 200 grams. There were epidemics of cholera, dysentery, typhoid fever and typhus. In addition to the military danger, the revolution was threatened by the decline in the physical strength of the population and the rampage of infectious diseases which were mowing down hundreds of thousands of people. "Typhus among a population that is exhausted by hunger, is ill, has no bread, soap or fuel," Lenin said with alarm, "may prove a calamity that will prevent our tackling any sort of socialist development."[1]

The Party undertook energetic measures to cope with the

[1] V.I. Lenin, *Collected Works*, Vol. 30, p. 185.

situation. The All-Russia Commission for Improving the Sanitary State of the Republic was set up. A concentrated effort to eradicate typhus and other infectious diseases, improve sanitation and draw working people into carrying out these measures were the first steps taken by the young Soviet health-protection system.

The basic principles of health protection were formulated in the Second Program of the Party. It envisaged "above all the implementation of large-scale health-building and sanitary measures with a view to preventing the development of diseases." These measures included sanitation of inhabited localities (protection of the soil, water and air); the organization of public catering on scientific hygienic principles and the enactment of legislation on sanitation. The Party regarded it as its immediate task to combat social diseases (tuberculosis, venereal diseases, alcoholism, etc.) and to organize free and qualified medical and pharmaceutical assistance accessible to all.

Of course, in the first years of Soviet power medical assistance could not always be provided because there was a shortage of doctors and medical establishments. Measures were taken to train medical personnel and build more hospitals and clinics. In 1928 the number of doctors and paramedical personnel increased nearly 2.5 times compared to 1913. By then such particularly dangerous diseases as smallpox, beubonic plague and cholera had been stamped out.

The first, second and third five-year plans marked important stages in radically improving the country's medical service. In 1929 the Central Committee of the Party adopted the resolution "On Medical Service to Workers and Peasants" and in 1931, the resolution "On Medical Personnel."

As the national income increased, more funds were allocated for the health service. The number of hospitals and clinics, medical schools and medical research institutions grew rapidly. Sanitation and disease-prevention work was carried out on an ever larger scale. The quality of medical assistance was improved. Out patient facilities were expanded, and medical rooms were set up at enterprises.

By the end of 1940 the USSR already had 155,000 doctors,

or almost 5.5 times the number in prerevolutionary Russia.

In the years of the Great Patriotic War, the Communist Party and the Soviet Government took measures to create the necessary conditions for treating the wounded. In addition to military hospitals, an extensive network of evacuation hospitals was organized far behind the lines. Large-scale work was conducted to safeguard the health of the civilian population. Dispensaries, first-aid rooms and even whole medical departments were opened at many enterprises. Large factories established after-work sanatoria which helped workers to keep in good health without discontinuing work. Emergency anti-epidemic commissions were formed everywhere to tighten medical control over sanitary conditions in the country. The Party's concern for the health of the military and civilian population was one of the important factors contributing to the victory of our people in the war.

In postwar years the question of improving the health service was discussed at all Party congresses. Concrete measures in this field were outlined in a number of joint decisions of the CPSU Central Committee and the USSR Council of Ministers. The adoption of the Fundamentals of Legislation on Health Protection in 1969 was of great social and political significance.

Economic progress makes it possible to increase allocations for the health service. In the past 15 years allocations rose by more than 150 percent. In 1980, they amounted to over 18 billion rubles, or roughly the same as the defense budget for that year.

During the years of socialist and communist construction, a nationwide network of medical establishments, from village dispensaries to specialized centers have been built in our country. More and more doctors and other medical personnel have been trained, and the standards of medical training have been steadily raised. Medical science and industry have been developing at an intensive pace. Hospitals and polyclinics are equipped with modern facilities. The production of medicines has increased, and extensive disease prevention measures have been carried out.

Under developed socialism a qualitatively new and ramified

health-protection system based on the latest achievements of the world medical science has been build in our country. The right of Soviet people to health protection has become a reality and is enshrined for the first time in the 1977 Constitution of the USSR.

What are the guarantees of this right?

In keeping with the Constitution, *the right to health protection is ensured first of all by free, qualified medical care provided by state health institutions.* This humane principle, introduced already in the first years of Soviet power, is the cornerstone of the socialist health protection system.

Every year the therapeutic and disease-prevention institutions of our country register more than two billion visits and calls by patients to doctors. When going to the doctor no one looks into his or her purse. All medical assistance, from simple bandaging to complicated surgery, is free. The state covers all expenses on the prevention and treatment of diseases. This is also true of expert medical consultations, calls for first aid and laboratory analyses and tests. One day's stay in a hospital or specialized clinic costs the state, on the average, no more than eight rubles.

In the capitalist countries, a large part of the health-protection system is a private business. In the United States, for instance, the population's expenses for medical assistance exceed those for the purchase of clothes and footwear. Surgery in a U.S. hospital, depending on the severity and length of the operation, can cost the patient 10,000 dollars and more. And people in the medical "business" continue to raise their charges for medical assistance. Because of this, it was pointed out in the U.S. press, half of the population in the United States do not seek doctors' help when they need it. Senator Edward Kennedy has noted in this connection that the health protection system in the United States is based on the chase for profits and ignores the needs of the people.

The right to health protection in the USSR is ensured by extension of the network of therapeutic and health-building institutions. There are about 60,000 such state-maintained institutions in the country, all provided with modern equipment. Their fixed assets amount to 35 billion rubles. In the past 15 years alone, the number of hospital beds has increased by nearly 50 percent to reach 3.3 million. The number of medical workers stands at six million, including a little less than a million doctors, 80 percent more than in 1965. More than one-third of the world's doctors work in the Soviet Union, which accounts for only six percent of the world's population. We have long since outstripped the capitalist countries in the number of doctors, hospital beds and other indicators per 10,000 residents.

Polyclinics and dispensaries are the principal link in the Soviet health-protection system. More than 80 percent of patients begin and complete treatment in these institutions. In our country medical assistance operates on a subdistrict principle. Districts served by one polyclinic are usually divided into subdistricts, each with an average population of 2,400. In addition to receiving patients in the polyclinic the subdistrict physicians make house calls and arrange expert consultations for patients when necessary.

In the countryside, too, a medical subdistrict is the center for rendering medical assistance. It is comprised of a hospital or a dispensary, midwifery and medical aid centers, maternity homes and nurseries for newborns. The number of people served by a rural medical sub-district averages 4,000.

In addition to the territorial therapeutic and disease prevention institutions, industrial enterprises have their own medical-sanitary departments, medical aid centers and after-work sanatoria.

The Soviet Constitution ensures the right to health protection by developing and improving safety and hygiene in industry.

All ministries and government departments are required to work out, in consultation with health-protection agencies and trade unions, comprehensive plans for sanitary and health building measures aimed at improving labor protection and safety engineering, preventing occupational diseases and reducing the incidence of occupational injury. More than two billion rubles is allocated by the state annually for these purposes.

All state-established standards for machines include safety engineering provisions. "Our goal," Leonid Brezhnev said, "can be formulated as follows: from safety rules to safe technology.

We have embarked on that road and will undeviatingly follow it."

There is strict control over the observance of labor protection and safety rules in all the branches of the national economy. In addition to specialists, this work is carried out by about four million volunteer public inspectors, members of labor protection commissions and nonstaff labor protection inspectors.

As a result, the incidence of industrial injury and occupational disease in our country is among the lowest in the world.

Disease prevention, early detection of diseases and large-scale health-building measures are leading trends in the Soviet health protection system. Every year more than 110 million people, especially children, expectant mothers, teenagers and students of secondary and higher schools, undergo health checkups.

A network of special outpatient clinics has been set up which perform medical checkups for the purpose of early detection and treatment of diseases, examine various groups of the population, organize highly qualified medical assistance and keep patients under regular observation. These institutions wage a planned campaign against such diseases as TB, cancer, nervous disorders, etc. The work is so organized that a patient registered at one of these medical institutions is under its constant care and is periodically examined by a physician who may also maintain contacts with his or her relatives if necessary, etc.

There exists in the USSR a system of health education institutions, including special schools for sanitary education. Doctors and medical scientists give hundreds of thousands of lectures at clubhouses and other community centers.

According to the USSR Constitution, the right to health protection is ensured by measures to improve the environment. This is a long-term problem which the Communist Party regards as a major socio-economic challenge. Great attention has been paid to it in recent years. "As we take steps to speed up scientific and technical progress," Leonid Brezhnev pointed out, "we must see to it that it should combine with the rational treatment of natural resources and should not cause dangerous air and water pollution or exhaust the soil."

For the first time in world constitutional practice, our Fundamental Law defines the responsibility of the state for the preservation of the environment. Measures are being taken to protect and to use scientifically and rationally the land and its mineral wealth, water resources and the plant and animal kingdoms, to preserve the purity of the air and water, to ensure the replenishment of natural riches and improve man's environment. In the 10th Five-Year Plan period alone, more than nine billion rubles was allocated for these purposes.

In our country the use of natural resources is subject to legislative control and there are rules for the protection of the environment. Specifically, the USSR Supreme Soviet has adopted the Fundamentals of Land and Water Legislation, the Fundamentals of Legislation on Mineral Wealth, and laws to protect atmospheric air and the animal kingdom.

The planning of inhabited localities and construction in these localities must meet strict sanitary standards. The interests of environmental protection are taken into consideration in drawing up plans for locating branches of the national economy, large industrial complexes, large recreation zones and nature preserves. Not a single enterprise is put into operation without waste-purification facilities.

In recent years the CPSU Central Committee has adopted a number of decisions on questions of environmental protection. These relate to improving our methods of protecting nature, the mineral wealth, forests, the Caspian, Black and Azov seas, the basins of the Volga and Ural rivers, and the wealth of Lake Baikal, etc.

Under the USSR Constitution the state is obliged to take special care of the health of the upcoming generation and prohibits juvenile labor that is not connected with job training at schools, in the family, or with subsidiary husbandry.

Children's polyclinics and consultation centers which work on the subdistrict principle register children of all ages who suffer from chronic diseases, observe with special care newborn babies and small children and conduct inoculation drives. Schoolchildren are looked after by school physicians.

In addition to the general medical institutions, there are about

1,200 sanatoria for children who require special care and medical observation. In recent years more sanatoria and therapeutic rest homes have been built where children live together with their parents, and also specialized sanatorium-type Young Pioneer camps which function all year round.

The constitutional right to health protection is guaranteed by developing research to prevent and reduce the incidence of disease and ensure citizens' long and active lives. Soviet medical scientists have at their disposal up-to-date research apparatus and instruments. Research programs have been undertaken in the spheres of cardiovascular, cancerous, virus, endocrinological and other diseases; protection of the health of mothers and children, scientific dietary principles; and environmental hygiene.

A great deal has been done in the field of public health in the Soviet period. Infantile mortality has dropped to one-tenth of the former level, and average life expectancy has risen from 32 years in the European, most highly developed, part of Russia at the end of the last century, to 70 years throughout the Soviet Union today.

The 25th Congress of the CPSU called concern for the health of Soviet people one of the most important socialist tasks. Great attention was paid to this question also by the 26th Congress. "Everything must be done," Leonid Brezhnev stressed, "to enable Soviet people to receive timely, skilled and considerate medical care always and everywhere."

FULLY PAID BY THE STATE AND SOCIETY

Citizens of the USSR have the right to maintenance in old age, in sickness and in the event of complete or partial disability or loss of the breadwinner. From Article 43 of the USSR Constitution.

At the beginning of this century the working people of Russia had no material maintenance in old age, in sickness, in the event of disability or unemployment.

Here is a typical request addressed to the manager of the Kharkov locomotive works, dated 1910:

". . . My husband Andrei Sidorov, who worked in the foundry shop of the locomotive works in your charge, fell gravely ill in February because of the very arduous work he had to do and died on April 13, leaving me with two small children without any means of subsistence . . . I beg you to show your great mercy and help a poor widow with children, lest we should be left without our daily bread."

The reply was: "No aid can be given."

The beggarly wages prevented workers from saving up for a rainy day. The demands of the working class in the sphere of social insurance, formulated in those years by the Communists, included insurance for all wage-earning and salaried workers, with the expenses involved to be borne by the entrepreneurs and the state, social maintenance for workers in all cases of disability, and complete self-administration in this sphere.

In 1912, alarmed by the intensity of the revolutionary movement, the czarist government rushed through a law on insuring workers in the event of illness or permanent injury. But the state insurance did not extend to agricultural and construction workers, railroad workers and seamen, and whole areas of the country (Siberia, the Far East, and Central Asia) remained outside the insurance scheme. No provision was made for old age and disablement. The biggest part of the insurance premiums was to be paid by the workers themselves, whose contributions were 50 percent higher than those of the entrepreneurs and claimed up to three per cent of earnings. Benefits were small and were paid only from the fourth day of the loss of working capacity and for a short period. The management of insurance was, to all intents and purposes, placed by law in the hands of entrepreneurs.

"I was a skilled worker, and my pay was higher than average. Once I fell ill and remained disabled for two months, and during all this time I received only 15 rubles from the insurance fund . . . Add to this the doctor's fees and the cost of medicines, and you will see in what position I, a skilled worker, found myself. The two months of illness left me a wreck." This story was told by Mikhail Kalinin, the first Soviet President.

The czarist insurance law roused the indignation of the proletariat. In Lenin's words, it was a law which rode "roughshod over the most vital interests of the workers."[1]

The Party exposed the essence of the bourgeois reforms which were designed to deceive the workers, explained to the masses of workers that the promulgation of insurance laws alone would not eliminate poverty, insecurity and lack of rights, and urged them to subordinate the struggle for social insurance to the general political struggle of the proletariat.

Immediately after the victory of the October Revolution the Party set about carrying out its social insurance program. The People's Commissariat for Labor was put in charge of its implementation.

Decrees were issued introducing state provision for the unemployed and insurance against illness, which covered the whole country, all branches of the economy and all employed persons. Pensions to workers who were victims of industrial accidents were doubled. The trade unions took an active part in establishing sick-pay funds for providing allowances for workers in the event of temporary disability, accidents, pregnancy and childbirth, and for rendering medical assistance to workers and their

[1] V.I. Lenin, *Collected Works,* Vol. 17, p. 477.

families. The funds were made up of obligatory contributions by entrepreneurs. Wage-earning and salaried workers were exempted from paying insurance dues.

The 16th Party Congress in 1930 pointed out that the trade unions should be the main agency in managing the vast social insurance funds and that the level of social maintenance should be more differentiated, account being taken of the importance of the work performed, seniority and a person's attitude to work. Central funds directly administered by the trade unions were established in the leading industries and in transport.

In 1933 all management of social insurance bodies, their funds and property were handed over to the trade unions. The categories of workers entitled to retirement pensions were broadened. Later this right was extended to all workers, technicians and engineers, and finally to office workers.

In the war years larger pensions were paid to all working pensioners irrespective of their earnings, thus providing incentives to many elderly but still able-bodied people for going back to work. Maximum temporary disability benefits were paid to working war invalids. Assistance was given to the families of servicemen.

An important social measure of the postwar period was the introduction of pensions for collective farmers. In 1964 the USSR Supreme Soviet passed a law on this matter, which was welcomed by collective farmers. Thus a uniform social maintenance system was established in the country.

The USSR Constitution guarantees to every citizen the right to maintenance in old age, in sickness and in the event of complete or partial disability or loss of the breadwinner.

Social insurance is extended automatically to every person as soon as he goes to work. No one is left without material maintenance. And no one pays anything. All expenses are covered by the state.

Social insurance funds are formed from payments by enterprises and institutions, whose size is determined by the government and amounts to from four to nine percent of the wage fund. There is a centralized fund for collective farmers, formed from each collective farm's payments.

The Soviet social insurance fund is used to pay allowances in the event of temporary disability (illness, injury, the need to look after a sick member of the family, a leave for sanatorium and health resort treatment, etc.), pregnancy, childbirth, the burial of a deceased worker or member of the family. It also pays old age and permanent disability pensions, allowances in the event of loss of the breadwinner and long-service bonuses. The fund also pays for sanatorium and health resort treatment and treatment in after-work sanatoria, for vouchers for holiday homes and tourist centers, for dietary purposes, for organizing children's recreation in Young Pioneer and health-building camps and for treatment in children's sanatoria.

Vast sums are spent for these purposes. In 1980, for instance, they amounted to 45.6 billion rubles, three times the 1965 figure and 48 times that of 1940. The amount paid is high and is raised systematically, in accordance with plan. Temporary disability benefits in the event of an industrial accident or occupational disease equal 100 percent of wages and are paid, as a rule, from the first day regardless of the length of service.

Such is the social insurance system in our country. The social security system in capitalist countries has many defects. In the West, social security funds are actually made up in large part of payments by the workers themselves and are often accessible only to those who have made such payments over a certain period. Disability pay rarely exceeds 50–60 percent of wages and is paid, not from the first day of illness, but upon the expiration of a "waiting period" lasting up to seven days.

In the Soviet Union the right to material maintenance is guaranteed, in keeping with the Constitution, by the provision by the state or by collective farms of retirement pensions, permanent disability pensions and pensions for the loss of the breadwinner.

Pensions make up the largest expenditure item in the Soviet social insurance budget—more than 70 percent. This is understandable. In 1980 the number of pensioners in our country reached 49.9 million, or 19 percent of the population, compared to four million, or two percent of the population in 1941.

Retirement pensions are provided to all working people who have reached a certain age and who have worked for a definite number of years. The retirement age for men is 60 years and the length of service, 25 years; for women, 55 and 20 years respectively. There are exceptions whereby the required service time is reduced by 5–10 years. This applies to those working underground and in other conditions harmful to health, in the Far North, etc. Retirement pensions equal from 50 to 100 percent of wages, and the lower the wages, the higher the percentage taken in computing pensions.

In most capitalist countries the retirement age is higher than in the USSR. In the United States, the FRG, the Netherlands and Sweden it is 63–65 years, and in Norway, 66 years. Moreover, considerable sums are deducted from wages and salaries as insurance dues (6.65 percent in the United States, 13.2 percent in the FRG).

The standard of living and the quality of the medical service in the USSR are such that almost one-third of pensioners continue to work, thus easing somewhat the shortage of labor in the country.

Disability pensions are paid in the event of permanent or prolonged loss of working ability. A certain length of service is required for this. However, those disabled as a result of industrial injury or occupational disease receive disability pensions irrespective of length of service, and the pensions are larger.

Pensions for loss of the breadwinner are paid to the fully dependent members of the deceased worker.

The Constitution guarantees employment for the partially disabled. It is the duty of the management of enterprises and institutions to provide these persons with jobs they can perform. If the enterprise or institution where a person worked prior to his disability has no such possibilities, social maintenance bodies are responsible for finding employment for him or her on the basis of recommendations of expert medical-labor commissions. Disabled persons have a shorter working day or working week, work in special shops or sections set up for the purpose, and they are given the necessary vocational training.

Maintenance through social insurance in the USSR is not fixed at a single level. Here account is taken of the size of a person's earnings, the length of his service and the particular working conditions. This fully accords with the principle "from each according to his ability, to each according to his work." Thus, the proposals put forward during the discussion of the draft of the Constitution that equal pensions be instituted for all or that their size be determined solely on the basis of length of service, without consideration for the qualifications of workers and the character of their work, were rejected.

The management of social insurance rests on a broad democratic basis. The bulk of the work here is done by local trade union committees. They approve the payment of benefits and allowances, issue vouchers for sanatoria, health resorts, holiday homes, tourist and health-building institutions and children's summer camps; check on the organization of the medical service, and see to the timely payment of social insurance dues by enterprises and institutions. Industrial and office workers take part in this work through their trade union commissions for social insurance. The trade unions' rights in this field are determined by legislation, which also fixes the size of allowances and other payments.

Pensions are appointed and disability is established directly by the state, that is, by agencies of the social maintenance ministries of the union republics, but the trade unions exercise control over this work.

The social security scheme is being constantly improved in the USSR. In accordance with the decisions of the 26th Congress of the CPSU, the minimal retirement and disability pensions for workers and collective farmers will be increased, and other measures will be taken to improve the social maintenance of the population. Concrete measures in this field are outlined in the joint decision of the CPSU Central Committee and the USSR Council of Ministers, "On Measures for Further Improving the Social Maintenance of the Population," adopted immediately after the 26th Congress. Our objective is gradual transition to society providing complete material security for persons who are no longer able to work.

THE HOUSING PROBLEM: HISTORY, POLICY, LAW

Citizen of the USSR have the
right to housing. From Article 44
of the USSR Constitution

The right of Soviet people to housing, as well as to health protection, is for the first time given legislative embodiment in the new USSR Constitution. This was made possible by the consistent implementation of a large-scale housing construction program.

The development of capitalism in Russia was accompanied by the rapid growth of cities. This led to a vast demand for housing, and by the beginning of this century the country was faced with an acute housing shortage. The majority of workers rented rooms and beds, with two or three families to a room, in cities or in suburban villages. From 100 to 200 people could be crowded into one lodging house with two or three tiers or bunks in a barracklike building put up by entrepreneurs. Married workers thought themselves lucky if they managed to get a corner with a curtain. The majority had neither mattresses, blankets nor pillows and used their clothes as bedding.

In 1912 almost 850,000 people in Moscow, or 70 percent of the city's population, lived in extremely crowded conditions, in basements and sheds. According to incomplete data, there were 150,000 "bed" tenants and 63,000 lived in basements; about two-thirds of single workers shared the rent of a single bed, sleeping in shifts. After an inspection tour of workers' dwellings the chairman of the sanitary commission of the State Duma (the old Russian Parliament) noted that "the living population in tenements in the Vyborg Quarter in St. Petersburg is more densely packed than the dead population in the cemetary."

The situation was even worse in other industrial cities. In 1912, almost half of the coal miners of the Donets Coal Basin lived in deep dugouts without floors or windows, about which journalists wrote that they were "lairs rather than human dwellings." The writer Maxim Gorky likened the hovels of the Baku oil workers to heaps of debris left by an earthquate and to dwellings of prehistoric man.

Of all the countries of Europe, Russia had the worst over-crowding in workers' dwellings; in terms of workers' housing Russia was at the level of the most backward colonial countries. Public utilities and amenities were in a most primitive state. Rent for just having a roof over one's head took 20–25 percent of a worker's family budget, and for a separate room or two rooms —40–60 percent. Moscow landlords received two-thirds of the rent as net profit. In 1914, when the housing shortage became particularly acute, about 5,000 large apartments with all the amenities were standing empty in the rich districts of the city.

Similar contrasts were to be observed in the countryside. While rich peasants (kulaks), merchants and priests built large houses with iron roofs, the poor lived in small huts with straw roofs and dirt floors. Many huts had primitive stoves without chimneys so that the smoke was let out through the door. In winter livestock lived in the same buildings as people.

The basic principles and directions of the Communist Party's housing policy were worked out by Lenin even before the October Revolution. He stressed, in particular, that "only by *abolishing private property in land and building cheap and hygienic dwellings can the housing problem be solved,*"[1] that "the proletarian state has to forcibly move a very poor family into a rich man's flat,"[2] and that the working people "can and must themselves ensure the *proper,* most strictly regulated and organized distribution of . . . housing . . . *in the interests of the poor.*"[3] He wrote that in the period of socialist construction "the letting of houses owned by the whole people to individual families presupposes the collection of rent, a certain amount of control, and the employment of some standard in allotting the housing," and

[1]V.I. Lenin, *Collected Works,* Vol. 24, p. 476.
[2]*Ibid.,* Vol. 26, p. 112.
[3]*Ibid.,* p. 114–115.

that "it will be possible to supply dwellings rent-free"[1] to every family only under communism.

Our Party tackled the housing problem immediately after the victory of the October Revolution. By its very first decrees the Soviet Government expropriated houses belonging to capitalists and the nobility and provided well-appointed housing to hundreds of thousands of workers. Low-paid workers and the families of servicemen fighting on the war fronts were exempted from paying rent. Landlords were forbidden to raise rents.

Of great importance in the implementation of the housing policy was the decree "On the Abolition of the Right of Private Ownership of Real Estate in Cities." In keeping with this decree both builtup and vacant plots of land and all large tenement houses were taken over by the state. Management of the expropriated houses was entrusted to committees elected at general meetings of tenants. The redivision of housing proceeded amidst a fierce struggle. The former landlords resorted to all means to hold on to their possessions. Former czarist officeholders and members of the middle bourgeoisie often seized control of municipalized houses and hindered the implementation of the decisions of the Soviet Government.

Of course redistribution of housing alone could not solve the housing problem. Large-scale housing construction had to be carried out, but there was no adequate economic basis for this. There was no building industry as such. After the Civil War the country concentrated its efforts on restoring industry, transport and agriculture. A few residential buildings were built mostly with the help of credits from the state.

As industrialization got under way the housing question assumed special urgency. The growth rates of housing construction lagged far behind the growth of the working class, and the average permitted floor space per person was reduced. The housing shortage further hampered the development of industry and the growth of production personnel. To solve the problem, in 1926 the Central Committee of the Party proposed

[1] *Ibid.*, Vol. 25, p. 439.

urgent measures such as setting up a permanent fund to finance housing construction, to coordinate housing construction plans with plans for the rehabilitation and development of major industrial centers, to increase the production of building materials and to reduce interest on credits and loans, etc.

It was necessary to build housing as quickly and as cheaply as possible, for funds were needed primarily for industrialization. In such conditions the emphasis was on building dwellings for short-term use. Thus, people who built the first giants of Soviet industry had to live in barracks, tents and even dugouts at first.

But as early as 1930, the 16th Party Congress called for going over to industrial methods of construction, forming permanent construction teams and building houses all year round. This marked the beginning of a qualitatively new stage in housing construction in the country. The building materials industry began to develop faster, and increasing quantities of machinery were supplied to the builders.

With the consolidation of the economy the state was able to pay for almost the entire cost of urban housing construction. The local Soviets and also enterprises and institutions which had houses under their administration were put in charge of the management of all state-owned housing, made responsible for technical and sanitary supervision and were given control over the maintenance and repair of buildings.

Housing legislation was being constantly improved in the first Soviet years. By the end of the 1920s, a system had emerged whereby the state covered the bulk of the expenditure on housing construction and maintenance, and the system has remained unchanged to this day.

By the standards of those years, the scale of housing construction in the country was vast indeed (in 1940 the stock of urban housing was 2.3 times greater than in 1913), but this was still insufficient, as the urban population was growing at an exceptionally fast rate, reaching 63 million on the eve of the Second World War. Thus the availability of housing remained limited, and in some regions the housing situation even worsened. Rooms were first allotted to employees of enterprises of key industries.

It should also be borne in mind that for all their importance the investments in housing construction were limited. The accelerated development of the heavy industry and the buildup of the country's defense potential (Hitler's Germany was preparing for war) demanded the strictest economy even where the prime necessities were concerned.

The war greatly aggravated the housing problem. The invaders destroyed and burned down 1,710 cities and industrial townships and more than 70,000 villages. Six million buildings were razed to the ground. In Byelorussia the fascists destroyed three-quarters of all housing. Kiev, Minsk, Stalingrad, Novgorod, Sevastopol and many other cities lay in ruins. About 25 million people were made homeless.

The law on the five-year plan for the rehabilitation and development of the national economy for 1946–1950 provided for the "restoration of destroyed housing in cities, industrial townships and villages that were under occupation, and organization of new housing construction on a scale ensuring a considerable improvement of the housing conditions of the people."

In the second half of the 1950s, standard projects began to resume again; many industrial enterprises began to build houses for their employes with the help of the state. Capital investments in housing construction rose steadily. They amounted to 33.4 billion rubles in 1961–1965 and 68.1 billion rubles in 1976–1980.

The capacities of building and assembly organizations were increased; the level of mechanization was raised; advanced technology and new, improved structures were introduced and fully prefabricated house-building was practiced on an ever wider scale.

It has become customary to prepare for tenancy approximately 100 million square meters of floor space every year. This is equivalent to the appearance, every month, of a new city with more than half a million residents.

The development of state and public (cooperative) housing construction is a reliable material guarantee of the right of Soviet people to housing. In the last 15 years the growth rates of housing have greatly exceeded the growth rates of the urban population. Every year about 11 million people have their housing conditions improved. For its scale of housing construction the Soviet Union takes the first place in the world.

By the end of 1980 all cities and urban-type settlements were receiving electricity; 89 percent had a piped water supply; 86 percent had central heating; 87 percent had sewerage systems; 55 percent had hot water; and 79 percent were supplied with gas. Individual homes, mostly one- and two- bedroom houses with auxiliary premises and outbuildings and kitchen gardens are being built in the countryside.

The right to housing is ensured by low rents and charges for utilities. The state provides housing free of charge. The rent rates have remained unchanged since 1928; on the average, rent plus the utility service charges come to about three percent of the family budget of a wage-earning or salaried worker. As for amenities, there is no comparison between what was available then and what we have today. Nowhere in the West do people pay so little for housing as in the USSR. In the Federal Republic of Germany, for instance, a skilled worker has to pay a third, or at least a quarter, of his earnings on housing. In other capitalist countries, rents take up 20–30 percent of the family budget. Tens of thousands of flats remain vacant in New York, London, Tokyo and other Western capitals because average citizens cannot afford them.

The USSR Constitution says that housing should be distributed under public control. The order in which a person registers for better housing, the provision of housing and the amount of floor space permitted per person are established by the state, but an important part in this work is played by the trade unions and other public organizations.

With more housing the state has to allocate more funds for its upkeep and for the provision of utilities. The tenants pay less than one-third of the cost involved.

In accordance with the Constitution, the state assists cooperative and individual house construction.

House-building cooperatives are set up under the executive committees of local Soviets as well as at enterprises, organizations and institutions. Citizens who need better housing may join a cooperative and receive an apartment for use in perpetuity. The state provides them with credits equalling 60–70 percent of the estimate construction cost, repayable over a period of 10–15 years. Construction of cooperative housing is included in the state plan for contract building-and-assembly work and the necessary materials and equipment are allocated. The state renders assistance to house-building cooperatives in the maintenance and repair of their houses and also helps in the construction and repair of individual houses and in improving their amenities.

Of great importance for ensuring the right to housing is the updating of legislation on housing. A big role is to be played in this by the Fundamentals of Housing Legislation of the USSR and the Union Republics.

It was noted at the 26th CPSU Congress that housing occupies a central place in our social program. Vast-scale housing construction will continue in our country.

III. RIGHTS AND FREEDOMS

CULTURE, EDUCATION, CREATIVE WORK

The Great October Socialist Revolution was a political and social revolution that in the conditions existing in Russia at that time proved to be the prelude to a cultural revolution. Accomplishment of the cultural revolution took place over a prolonged time.

The Communist Party took the position that a new culture could not be created out of nothing, in isolation from all the material and spiritual values of the past. They fought resolutely against those who wanted a "pure proletarian culture," talk of which Lenin called "nonsense."[1] Lenin pointed out that the task of the new society in the cultural field was not to invent some special culture, but "to gain possession of the culture that was created by the old social relations and has remained as the material basis of socialism."[2]

The task was to use the heritage of the past correctly, critically, in a truly responsible way, not to omit anything of value and at the same time "not to cram your mind with useless lumber,"[3] to take from every national culture only its democratic and socialist elements.

[1]V.I. Lenin, *Collected Works*, Vol. 31, p. 287.
[2]*Ibid.*, Vol. 27, p. 301.
[3]*Ibid.*, Vol. 31, p. 288.

In implementing a cultural revolution the Party set about the threefold task of eliminating the reactionary content of bourgeois-landowner culture, mastering all the cultural achievements of the past and placing them at the service of the people and building a socialist culture on this basis.

Lenin's program of the cultural revolution envisaged both the training of a new people's intelligentsia, and the securing of the cooperation of specialists who received their professional training before the revolution and who represented that heritage of technology and culture without which, Lenin said, the building of communism would not be possible. The Communist Party and the Soviet government exerted great efforts to win over the old intelligentsia, gradually drawing it into the building of a new life. Understandably, such a policy won over ever greater numbers of specialists who began to abandon their position of hostility and distrust and their wait-and-see attitude, and began to take an active part in the building of a new society, including the training of cadres of the new intelligentsia from among the workers and peasants. Already in 1936, speaking at an All-Union Congress of Soviets, V.L. Komarov, Vice President of the USSR Academy of Sciences, said that "the Soviet intelligentsia is an entirely new intelligentsia, an intelligentsia that serves the people."

FROM ILLITERACY TO UNIVERSAL COMPULSORY SECONDARY EDUCATION

> Citizens of the USSR have the right to education. From Article 45 of the USSR Constitution.

Nearly four-fifths of czarist Russia's adult population could neither read nor write. There were only 67 per 1,000 residents attending schools of some type. In a country with a population of 160 million, only about 290,000 people (less than 0.2 percent) had a higher, incomplete higher or specialized secondary education. There were only a few literate persons among many non-Russian peoples, and more than 40 nationalities had no written language of their own.

At the beginning of the century the journal *Vestnik vospitaniya,* commenting on the outlook of cultural development in Russia, said that it would take 180 years to achieve universal literacy among the country's male population and 280–300 years among the female population. There were sufficient grounds for such a prognosis. Allocations for education were much smaller than for the maintenance of prisons and the police. Education was a privilege of the ruling classes. Ananyeva, a peasant woman who was arrested for taking part in the revolutionary movement, wrote in her evidence that she had dreamed of sending her son to a secondary school. After reading her testimony Czar Alexander III commented: "That's what's so terrible: peasants trying to enter secondary school!" The Ministry of Public Education issued a special circular prohibiting the admission to secondary school of "children of coachmen, lackeys, cooks, laundresses, small shopkeepers and the like, whose children should on no account strive to have a secondary or higher education."

The working people's demands in the sphere of education were stated in the First Program of our Party. They included "free and obligatory universal general and vocational education of all children of both sexes aged under 16; provision by the state to the children of poor parents with meals, clothing and study aids," and "the right of the population to get an education in their native language, ensured by the establishment by the state and self-government bodies of schools necessary for this." The Party regarded the realization of these demands as being linked with its immediate political task of overthrowing the czarist autocracy and replacing it with a democratic republic.

In accordance with one of the first decrees issued by the Soviet Government a People's Commissariat for Education was formed which was put in charge of all primary, secondary, higher, private and special educational establishments in the country. The decree "On the Rules of Admission into Institutions of Higher Learning" provided access to higher education for children of workers and peasants. Education in higher schools became free, monthly allowances were paid to needy students and members of the propertied classes were deprived of all privileges in the field of education.

The Party's top-priority task was to put an end to illiteracy among the adult population.

It was a formidable task. It involved teaching many million people, evolving written languages for the nationalities that did not have them, and overcoming numerous national, religious and other prejudices. This work was started in the years of the Civil War and foreign military intervention. In January 1919 a decree was adopted "On Eliminating Illiteracy Among the Population of the Russian Federation." All inhabitants of the republic between 8 and 50 who could not read and write were obliged to attend literacy classes which were conducted either in their own native languages or in Russian, according to their wishes.

So many people were illiterate that the problem could not be solved by the efforts of professional teachers, and the Party called on all who could to contribute to the literacy campaign. An All-Russia Extraordinary Commission for the Elimination of Illiteracy was set up under the government and a society called "Down with Illiteracy" was organized. An active part in this movement was taken by Party, Komsomol and trade union organizations, commissions for work among women and many persons prominent in the sphere of the new, socialist culture. The public education agencies were empowered to draw the entire literate population into this work, by labor conscription. For those attending literacy classes the working day was reduced by two hours, with no cuts in pay.

There was a shortage of pens, pencils, paper, fuel for heating school rooms, electricity, school equipment and study aids. Often writing had to be done on posters and newspapers with charcoal or ink made from beet root or soot. But there was nowhere in the country where people were not studying. About three million people were taught to read and write in just one year.

The foundations of a system of adult education were laid in the course of the literacy campaign. Schools with a 10-month term of instruction at the level of the first two years of primary school and schools for semiliterates, providing complete primary education, were set up. Also in those years the first advanced schools were organized for adults whose curricula were similar to those secondary schools.

Immediately after the revolution, extensive work began to establish a network of primary and secondary schools. School communes were set up for orphans. The Communist Party and the Soviet Government worked persistently to enroll all children of school age in educational institutions.

Many teachers, especially those at primary schools, who were close to the people, welcomed the new government and supported the Communists' ideas and actions in the public education sphere. But most of the teachers at secondary schools, especially educators trained before the revolution, adopted a hostile attitude. Their mouthpiece, the journal *Pedagogicheskaya mysl,* said in 1921 that the establishment of the new Soviet school was one of the greatest calamities that had ever befallen Russian education.

However, what was being accomplished by the Soviet Government in the field of education and the Party's concern for the prestige, material well-being and living conditions of the teachers ("Our schoolteacher should be raised to a standard he has never achieved, and cannot achieve, in bourgeois society"[1]) were not without effect. It was stated in a declaration adopted by the First All-Union Congress of Teachers (1925): "We shall always and everywhere be loyal supporters of Soviet power and the Communist Party in their world-historic work, for we know now that the Party's cause is the cause of the entire working mankind."

The higher education system was being radically reformed although a section of reactionary-minded educators and professors did all they could to deny working people access to knowledge. In the first years of Soviet power it was, of course, difficult to enroll young workers and peasants in higher schools, for the lacked the requisite general educational preparation. Thus, in 1919, on Lenin's initiative, the so-called workers' faculties were organized at higher schools. They provided capable young people with a secondary education. By the 1925–26 academic year, one out of every four students in a higher school was a graduate of these faculties. By the 10th anniversary of the revolution (1927), the country had 148 higher schools and 1,037 specialized secondary schools, with an enrollment of 168,500 and 189,400 respectively, which was 1.5 and 5.3 times more than before the First World War.

The Party and the state also took steps to train skilled workers. In 1920 new types of vocational-technical schools were opened, which were attached to factories. They were the so-called factory schools.

But despite the progress made in the field of education and especially in the sphere of eliminating illiteracy, the country was still faced with a shortage of skilled personnel. On the initiative of the Party Central Committee, all work in the educational field was reorganized in accordance with a single plan and based on the pooling together of resources and funds and self-help. Illiteracy in the USSR had been virtually eliminated by the eve of the Second World War.

Many new schools were built in the 1930s. In keeping with the decisions of the 16th Party Congress (1930), universal compulso-

[1]V.I. Lenin, *Collected Works*, Vol. 33, p. 464.

ry primary education was introduced for children ages 8 to 15 who had not received primary schooling. This "granting to all young people an equal opportunity to have the right to develop their mental abilities" (Gorky) was implemented within three years. By 1932 almost all children between 8 and 11 were attending school. Universal compulsory, seven-year education was introduced in industrial cities, districts and townships.

The 18th Party Congress (1939) outlined an important five-year program for the further development of public education. It envisaged the introduction of universal secondary education in the cities of the Russian Federation and of seven-year schooling in the countryside and in all the national republics and bringing the number of pupils in general educational schools to 40 million and that of higher school students to 650,000. The program could not be implemented because of the war.

During the war years measures were taken to ensure the uninterrupted functioning of schools in the rear, in front-line areas and in partisan-controlled territories. Night schools were organized for those young people who could not attend regular schools. The network of higher, specialized secondary and vocational schools continued to function. They graduated 302,000 specialists with a higher education, 540,000 specialists with a specialized secondary education and almost 2.5 million skilled workers.

The war played havoc with the public education system in the temporarily occupied territories. The fascist invaders burned down, destroyed and sacked 82,000 secondary schools, 334 higher schools and a large number of specialized secondary and factory schools.

In the course of postwar socialist and communist construction the Party and government took measures to rapidly restore and further develop the entire system of public education. The main trends of this development were mapped out by Party congresses.

In accordance with the Constitution of the USSR, the right to education is ensured by the institution of universal compulsory secondary education for young people. We have been advancing steadily toward this goal from one five-year period to another, developing and strengthening the material and technical base of public education, extending the training of teachers and taking measures to improve the educational process. The latter half of the 1940s saw the completion, for the most part, of the transition to compulsory seven-year education; the transition to universal compulsory eight-year education was completed in the early 1960s and to universal compulsory secondary 10-year education in the 1970s. In the 1979–80 academic year, 99.2 percent of young people attended various types of schools providing a secondary education.

Today 80 percent of the people employed in the national economy have a higher or secondary (10-year or 8-year) education. One-hundred million two hundred thousand people are studying somewhere or another. In the past 15 years 60.3 million young people received a secondary or specialized secondary education. The USSR ranks first in the world for the educational level of the population. The leading role in the secondary education system belongs to *general schools:* 68.5 million out of the 88.2 million people who received a general or specialized secondary education in the period from 1918 to 1979 graduated from secondary general schools.

The right to education is guaranteed also by the broad development of vocational education. Since it was founded the state system of vocational training has become the main base for training skilled workers for all branches of the national economy. In 1959, vocational training was placed on a uniform general educational basis, i.e., an eight-year education. Somewhat earlier, technical schools were established for graduates of secondary general schools.

As part of the transition to universal secondary education, secondary vocational schools whose pupils receive a complete secondary education while learning a trade were opened. In the past 10 years the number of such schools has increased tenfold. Today they are attended by more than two million young people. The network of technical schools has also grown. Today 90 percent of young people pursuing a technical education attend secondary vocational and technical schools.

A big role in the public education system is played by specialized secondary schools, which enroll young people who have had at least an eight-year schooling in secondary general educational schools. There they receive not only a complete secondary education but also specialized training, and after graduation they are given posts as leading junior technicians in industry and agriculture. In 1980 the country had about 4,400 specialized secondary schools with more than 4.6 million students.

Institutions of higher learning are the concluding link in the public-education system. In 1980, there were 883 higher schools in the country, with a total enrollment of more than 5.2 million. Every year about 800,000 graduates of higher school receive diplomas as specialists with the highest qualification. The USSR has long ago outstripped the leading capitalist countries in the level and scale of higher education.

The Soviet public education system also includes evening and correspondence schools for young industrial and agricultural workers and evening and correspondence departments attached to specialized secondary and higher schools. Enrollment in them does not involve interrupting one's work. In the 1980–81 academic year about 8.7 million people studied in such schools and departments.

In the past few years the CPSU Central Committee and the Soviet Government have adopted a number of decisions concerning all the links of the public education system: "On the Further Improvement of the Training and Education of Pupils of General Schools and Their Preparation for Work," "On the Further Development of Higher School Education and Improvement of the Quality of Specialists' Training," "On Measures to Further Improve the Direction of Specialized Secondary Schools and the Quality of the Training of Specialists with a Specialized Secondary Education," and "On the Further Improvement of the Process of Training and Education of Pupils in the Vocational-Training System."

Much attention was paid by the 26th Congress of the CPSU to questions of the further development of the public education system and improvement of the quality of education and training.

Under the USSR Constitution, all types of education are free.

Education at all levels, from general schools to post-graduate courses is financed by the social consumption funds. The annual state expenditure per student from these funds is more than 180 rubles in general schools, over 680 rubles in specialized secondary schools and upwards of 1,000 rubles in higher schools. In addition, students of higher and specialized secondary schools receive monthly allowances and enjoy other benefits. Allowances are paid, as a rule, to students making normal progress, and these account for more than 70 percent of the students of specialized secondary and higher schools. Nearly all in need of housing live in hostels, paying a token sum of 1 ruble and 50 kopecks (the cost of six ice cream cones) per month. Educational establishments have lunchrooms and canteens where meals are much cheaper than in the ordinary city ones.

Great privileges are enjoyed by those studying without discontinuing work. To take tests and examinations and to prepare graduation theses they are given additional leaves of up to 40 days with full pay; for those enrolled in educational establishments situated in other cities the state pays half the fare to and from their college or university. Post graduate students at correspondence and evening educational establishments can have one additional day off per week while retaining 50 percent of their pay for that day.

In the USSR all have equal opportunities to get an education. Herein lies an important difference between the USSR and capitalist countries in the educational field. For example, according to a report prepared by the College Entrance Examination Board (USA), in the past 10 years average tuition fees in U.S. colleges have risen by 70 percent, and in some cases up to 10,000 dollars per year. Forty percent of young men and 60 percent of young women from families of what is called "low socioeconomic status" simply cannot afford this. Added to this is the crisis of U.S. secondary education, characterized by insufficient funds the declining quality of instruction, unruly classes, the despair of teachers and the apathy of the pupils. Today one in every four pupils leaves school before graduation.

The example of the USSR shows what can be achieved in the field of education under socialism.

ACCESS TO CULTURE

> Citizens of the USSR have the
> right to enjoy cultural benefits.
> From Article 46 of the USSR
> Constitution.

The world-famous Tretyakov Art Gallery in Moscow was opened to the general public before the October Revolution, but at that time it was visited by not more than 300 people daily (today the figure is more than 4,000). The collections of the Hermitage Museum in St. Petersburg were inaccessible to the masses altogether. As its last prerevolutionary director declared: "The very idea that the museum should provide a source of aesthetic enjoyment for the masses of the people is too absurd for words."

The position of the theater in czarist Russia can be judged from the fact that a number of theatres were controlled by the Ministry of the Imperial Court (the so-called imperial theaters), and the rest were controlled by the police. Book publishing was a private enterprise.

"Tolstoy, the artist, is known to an infinitesimal minority, even in Russia," Lenin noted bitterly. "If his great works are really to be made the possession of all, a struggle must be waged against the system of society which condemns millions and scores of millions to ignorance, benightedness, drudgery and poverty—a socialist revolution must be accomplished."[1]

The Communist Party and the Soviet Government not only declared that the achievements of culture belonged to the entire people, but did everything to enable workers and peasants to really enjoy cultural benefits.

In the very first months of Soviet power the country's museums, including the Tretyakov Gallery and the Hermitage Museum, and all the largest private art collections were nationalized.

[1] V.I. Lenin, *Collected Works*, Vol. 16, p. 323.

Scores of monuments of architecture and objects of art became the property of the state. Many former palaces and country estates of the nobility around Petrograd (formerly St. Petersburg) and Moscow were turned into museums.

In the first postrevolutionary years, in an effort to introduce the masses of the people to cultural values, the Soviet state abolished entrance fees for museums and theaters. Despite the tremendous financial and economic difficulties facing the country, measures were taken to ensure the normal functioning of museums, art galleries, libraries and other cultural institutions. It is noteworthy that at the very height of the Civil War (November 1919) the government discussed the question of heating them.

The working people made wide use of the possibility of free access to art treasures. In 1919 alone Moscow's museums were visited by 500,000 people.

Everything was done to preserve cultural values, to save them from destruction and plunder. Already in November 1917, on instructions from Lenin, an agency in charge of museum affairs and for the protection of historical and art treasures was set up and decrees were issued "On Prohibiting the Taking out of the Country or Selling Abroad Objects of Exceptional Artistic and Historic Importance," "On the Registration and Protection of Historical and Art Treasures in the Possession of Private Individuals, Societies and Institutions," "On the Protection of Libraries and Book Depositories," and others. In 1918–1920 the state registered more than 550 old country estates, about 1,000 private collections and almost 200,000 works of art. Hundreds of owners of country estates and of the more valuable collections received certificates of government protection.

M.N. Pokrovsky, Deputy People's Commissar for Education, wrote at that time: "The country goes barefoot, but the Hermitage remains, during the revolution and thanks to it, the leading collection in the world after the Louvre and the Vatican . . . Some day a monument to the Russian proletarian will be erected in front of both the Academy of Sciences and the Academy of Arts because it was he, kept away by his hard past from science and the arts, about which he presumably knew nothing, who prevented these rare hothouse plants in our conditions from perishing in critical moments, who warmed and nursed them for the future generations while himself suffered from hunger and cold."

Today *concern for the protection of art treasures and cultural and historical monuments is a constitutional duty of the Soviet state.*

More than 150,000 monuments of history, archeology and architecture are under the protection of the state. Large scale work is being conducted to collect objects of fine art and applied art, utensils of historical and artistic interest and folk songs and stories. New museums dedicated to the works of outstanding writers, composers, artists and actors are being established. The state allocates vast sums for restoration work. Not only individual monuments are being restored, but whole architectural ensembles and even towns, among them such world-famous ones as Suzdal, Bukhara, Samarkand and Khiva.

Special mention should be made of the restoration of cultural and historical monuments destroyed by the fascist invaders during the 1941–1945 Great Patriotic War. The palaces of Pavlovsk, Pushkin and Petrodvorets, ancient monuments in Smolensk, Pskov and Novgorod and the Pushkin memorial museum in the village of Mikhailovskoye were restored from ruins and ashes.

Active work is being conducted by the societies for the protection of historical and cultural monuments. The Constitution says: "Concern for the preservation of historical monuments and other cultural values is a duty and obligation of citizens of the USSR."

That is how we do things in our country, and it is hard for Soviet people to comprehend such facts as, for instance, the reallocation, for the upkeep of the San Vittore prison, of 200 million lire originally earmarked by the Italian government for the renovation of the Brera Gallery in Milan, which is in bad repair, with leaky roofs over halls hung with pictures by Titian, Raphael, Veronese and other great masters.

It should be noted that Soviet power inherited a poor material basis of working people's culture from old Russia. For instance, in 1913, there were only 14,000 libraries in the country with a total of 9.4 million books (6 books per 100 people).

Immediately after it was formed, the workers' and peasants' state began to take measures to strengthen the material basis of cultural development. It was stated in the Party's Second Program that one of the urgent tasks in this sphere was "all-round assistance by the State in the field of self-education and self-development of workers and peasants (the establishment of a network of institutions of public education outside the school system: libraries, schools for adults, people's clubhouses and universities, courses, lectures, cinema houses, art studios, etc.)."

To put an end to the "book hunger," the paper industry and the largest publishing and printing houses were nationalized. The Communist Party and the Soviet Government paid much attention to the matter of radically reorganizing book publishing in the interests of socialist construction. The decree on state publishing houses in December 1917 said that, alongside textbooks and political and other special literature, there should be published cheap editions of works by classical authors that most people could afford.

One of the first cultural undertakings of the young Soviet state was the publication, beginning from 1918, on Maxim Gorky's initiative, of the "World Literature" series. The series included translations of works of Persian, Turkish, Arabian, Chinese and Japanese literature, and works by Byron, Dickens, Scott, Heine, Voltaire, Balzac, Stendhal and many other writers of Europe and America. Commenting on this initiative, Romain Rolland wrote: "A series of very carefully produced works by the classical authors of Russian and world literature is being published—and sold at a very low price . . . The state loses money on this publishing venture and knows it. But it thinks nothing of it. It wants the people to read. And it is succeeding in this. The people read unbelievably much."

As early as 1918–1919, about 500 books by classical authors of Russian and foreign literature, textbooks and other publications appeared. But this was still not enough. In the middle of 1921 the quantity of paper available in the Soviet republic was only four percent of that available in czarist Russia in 1914. Even wrapping paper was used. In such conditions it was necessary to organize rational and effective utilization of the available stocks of paper. The Soviet government nationalized private libraries, with the exception of those of scientists and workers in literature and the arts. The millions of books thus obtained went to scientific and public libraries.

As the economic position of the USSR improved, the number of publishing houses grew. With each year more books were published and the network of libraries expanded. In 1940 there were 95,400 public libraries with a total stock of about 200 million books.

Particularly noticeable were the successes of book publishing in the national republics. In 1937, as compared with 1913, the output of books in the Russian language increased 6.7 times, while that of books in the languages of other peoples of the USSR, 21 times. On the eve of the Great Patriotic War all the union Republics had reached just about the same level in the availability of libraries, and book funds had grown considerably everywhere.

After the revolution all theaters were nationalized and then reorganized in the interests of the new mass audiences. Numerous national theaters were opened. Vast importance was attached to the cinema. By 1940, the number of film projection units had risen to 28,000.

Newspaper publishing developed particularly rapidly. In 1940, 8,806 newspapers were published in the country with a total circulation of 38.4 million (in contrast with the 859 newspapers with a total circulation of 2.7 million in 1913). The large force of nonstaff, worker and peasant correspondents grew steadily, forming an efficient link between the press and the masses.

In the latter half of the 1920s, regular radio broadcasting began. Just before the Great Patriotic War Soviet radio broadcasting reached nearly 400,000 hours annually. The number of radio sets in the country exceeded one million.

The revolution brought forth such entirely new centers of culture as recreation and reading rooms at enterprises, workers' and peasants' clubs, traveling libraries, cultural propaganda trains and steamships, etc. In 1940 there were 118 clubhouses and houses and palaces of culture.

Thus, in the prewar period the sound material basis for a new, socialist culture was laid in our country.

In the war years cultural institutions, like the whole national economy, suffered tremendous damage. The invaders pillaged and destroyed more than 100 million books belonging to public libraries alone and razed thousands of libraries, museums, theaters and clubhouses to the ground. Restoration of cultural establishments became a top-priority task in the cultural sphere after the war. The trade unions, the Komsomol, cooperatives and broad masses of the population participated in this patriotic undertaking.

Subsequently the material and technical base of culture was steadily broadened and strengthened. More and more funds from the state budget and other sources went into education, cultural-enlightenment work and the development of art.

The USSR Constitution says that the right of Soviet people to enjoy cultural benefits is ensured by broad access to the cultural treasures of national and world culture that are preserved in state and public collections; by the development and fair distribution of cultural and educational institutions throughout the country; by developing television and radio broadcasting and the publishing of books, newspapers and periodicals; and by extending the free library service. In 1980, there were 607 theatres, more than 1,500 museums, 137,000 clubhouses and houses and palaces of culture, and 152,000 film projection units in the Soviet Union. According to UNESCO data, the USSR holds first place in the world for the number of visits to places of cultural entertainment. In 1980, for instance, the number of visits to theaters was 120 million; to museums, 156 million; and to motion-picture theaters, 4.3 billion.

Also according to UNESCO data, Soviet people read more than people anywhere else in the world. Since the revolution, 52 billion copies of books and booklets have been published in the USSR, and the publication of scientific and political literatures and fiction continues to grow. In 1980 alone, about 80,000 titles of books and booklets with a total print of 1.8 billion copies were published, with fiction and books on art making up one half of this number.

At present we have 132,000 public libraries with a total of 1.8 billion books. There are more than 700 million books in the libraries of general schools and over two billion in scientific, technical and other special libraries. More than half of the country's population use the services of public libraries. In addition, there are more than 30 billion books and booklets in personal libraries. Every year 700–800 million books are added to these libraries. But, nevertheless, the population's demand for books is not yet fully satisfied.

In 1980 more than 13,000 newspapers, magazines and other periodicals were published in the USSR. There were over 200 publishing houses and two news agencies. The annual circulation of magazines and other periodicals had reached 3.2 billion and the daily circulation of newspapers, 173 million. On the average there are about six newspapers, magazines and other periodicals per family.

The entire territory of the Soviet Union is covered by radio broadcasting, and more than four-fifths of the population can see telecasts.

An important constitutional guarantee of the right of Soviet citizens to the enjoyment of cultural benefits is the extension of cultural exchanges with other countries. In keeping with the Helsinki Final Act we encounter cultural exchanges in every way and conclude inter-government agreements on such exchanges. The USSR maintains cultural contacts with 120 countries.

In the years of Soviet power books by authors from 136 countries have been published in the USSR. The number of titles of these works is 77,500 and the total printing, 2.4 billion copies. According to UNESCO figures, the USSR puts out five times more translated books than Britain and twice more than Japan, the United States and France. Translations of new works by contemporary foreign writers are regularly published in the *Inostrannaya Literatura* (Foreign Literature) monthly, which has a circulation of 600,000.

The international ties of the Soviet art world are being steadily extended. Forty large, foreign art exhibitions were held in the USSR from 1977–1979. They included exhibitions of American paintings of the second half of the 19th and the 20th centuries and pictures from the Georges Pompidou National Art and Culture Center in France and from the collection of the Royal Academy of Arts in London.

At present 130 plays based on works by foreign authors are being staged in Soviet theaters. In recent years theaters from France, the FRG, Britain, Italy, Canada, Greece and other countries, the opera and ballet troupes of Milan, Stockholm, Vienna, Paris and Stuttgart and symphony orchestras from Britain, the Netherlands and France have toured the Soviet Union. In 1980 alone, the USSR played host to more than 130 foreign theatrical companies and musical groups, which gave over 6,000 performances in more than 170 cities.

Every year the USSR buys and widely shows approximately 60 films from socialist countries and as many films from capitalist and developing countries. International film festivals are regularly held in our country. In the past few years Soviet TV viewers have seen a number of Western telefilms and serial programs.

It will be noted that films from capitalist countries make up about 10 percent of all films shown in the USSR, while films of all socialist countries account for only five percent of foreign films shown in the West. Films bought by the United States from us are shown in small cinemas, without proper publicity and press reviews. It's the same in the FRG, Italy and Britain.

It would seem that the opponents of détente fear a broadening of cultural contacts with the socialist countries, that they are doing everything to prevent working people in capitalist countries from getting to know about art under socialism. On the other hand, in the guise of cultural exchange, they try to foist upon the socialist countries "wares" that glamorizes violence, pornography, racism, acts of aggression, etc. Quite understandably, we are against this kind of "freedom of cultural exchange." This is in full accord with the letter and spirit of the Helsinki

Conference. We have never made a secret of the fact that our country welcomes only those works of art which are permeated with the ideas of humanism and democracy and serve to strengthen mutual understanding and trust among nations.

FREEDOM OF CREATIVE WORK

> Citizens of the USSR . . . are guaranteed freedom of scientific, technical, and artistic work. From Article 47 of the USSR Constitution.

Cultural values are the creation of human hands, intellect and talent. "The people are not merely the force which has created all material values," Maxim Gorky wrote, "they are the exclusive and inexhaustible source of spiritual values; in time, beauty and genius, they are, collectively, the first and foremost philosopher and poet, creator of all the great poems that exist, all the tragedies in the world, and, greatest among these tragedies, the history of world culture."[1]

The culture of developed socialism is deeply rooted in the people. For the first time in humanity's history, the Great October Socialist Revolution removed the shackles on talents "so abundant among the people whom as Lenin put it, "capitalism crushed, suppressed and strangled in thousands and millions."[2] It not only provided to working people broad access to the treasures of culture, but enabled them to become creators of cultural values and opened up unlimited opportunities for the

[1]Maxim Gorky, *On Literature*, Progress Publishers, Moscow, 1973, p. 71.
[2]V.I. Lenin, *Collected Works*, Vol. 26, p. 404.

display of their creative forces, capabilities and endowments. To use the words of Marx and Engels, in our country, "anyone in whom there is a potential Raphael" is "able to develop without hindrance."[1]

The Communist Party has always concerned itself with accomplishing this creative task of the cultural revolution. Under developed socialism, freedom of creative work has become an inalienable constitutional right of every Soviet citizen.

Freedom of scientific creative work in the USSR is guaranteed above all by broadening scientific research. The number of scientific workers in our country at present is about 1.4 million, of whom 435,000 hold degrees of doctors or candidates of science.

We began at an exceedingly low level. Not long before the First World War, after carrying out a study of the position of the Russian Academy of Sciences, one member of the State Duma said: "Had I not seen it with my own eyes, I would have hardly believed that in our capital, in the city of Peter the Great, on the bank of the Neva, such an attitude to science and to its shrine, the Academy, is possible . . . There is little difference between an academician and a village teacher in their working conditions, and it's hard to say which of the two had more comfortable conditions to work in."

The revolution marked a qualitatively new stage in the development of science in the country, turning it into a major factor in the economic, social and cultural transformation of society. Even in the years of the Civil War and economic dislocation, great attention was paid to the building of a network or research, academic and sectoral scientific establishments. State allocations for research were increased considerably.

Under the Party's guidance, scientific institutions conducted systematic studies of the country's natural resources, and carried out research on the rational distribution of productive forces, the electrification of industry, agriculture and transport and the reorganization of the national economy on the basis of the lastest technology.

In 1925 a system of postgraduate courses was established and

[1] Karl Marx, Frederick Engels, *The German Ideology*, Progress Publishers, Moscow, 1964, p. 430.

became the leading form of training scientific personnel. With every year more funds were earmarked for the development of science and an expansion of the material and technical basis of research. The activities of the Academy of Sciences acquired a fundamentally different character and scope. Its role in solving major economic problems increased noticeably after the government adopted, in 1925, a resolution "On Recognizing the Russian Academy of Sciences as the Highest Scientific Institution of the USSR".

Already in the 1920s, on the basis of research and sectoral institutes and laboratories, a single nationwide network of scientific centers and institutions was created. By 1929, the number of scientific establishments, including higher schools, had reached 1,400 and the number of scientific workers, 43,000. This was an important prerequisite for the reshaping of the national economy on the basis of the latest achievements in science and technology.

The outlays for science increased manyfold in the 1930s. In 1940, there were 2,359 scientific institutions in the country (including higher schools), and the number of scientific workers reached 98,300. Almost half of the scientific institutions were to be found in the national republics.

In the very first months of the war, measures were taken to evacuate the main scientific organizations from the western to the eastern part of the country. As a result, despite the tremendous damage inflicted on our science (the German fascist invaders destroyed 605 research institutes), the scientific potential of the country was not only preserved, but also strengthened. In the war years Soviet research institutes and laboratories successfully dealt with problems of improving military equipment, carried out work of prospecting for and reclaiming natural resources in the east of the country and developed new medicines. Fundamental theoretical research also continued.

In the postwar period, research was started in a number of new spheres of natural, technical and social sciences, with great attention being paid to strengthening the country's defense capacity. August 1949 saw the end of the nuclear monopoly of the West. In 1948 the first Soviet long-range guided ballistic missile was launched; in 1950 the first Soviet electronic computer was built; in 1954 the world's first atomic power station was commissioned in our country.

The requirements of the country's socioeconomic development and the scientific and technological revolution that unfolded on a broad scale in the mid-fifties were the main factors contributing to the rapid growth of the network of scientific institutions and of the number of scientific workers in the subsequent decades. In 1980 the outlays for science were 21.3 billion rubles, thrice the 1965 figure.

The Constitution of the USSR makes it a duty of the socialist state to ensure planned development of science, the training of scientific personnel, and introduction of the results of scientific research in the national economy and other areas of life.

The Communist Party, it was noted at the 26th CPSU Congress, holds that the building of a new society is unthinkable without science. The CPSU Central Committee calls for further enhancing the role and responsibility of the USSR Academy of Sciences, for improving the organization of the entire system of scientific research, for a more caring attitude to the needs of science.

The CPSU orients Soviet scientists to extending and deepening the investigation of the laws governing the development of nature and society, to solving pressing problems of accelerating scientific and technical progress and increasing efficiency of production, and to raising the material and cultural standards of the people. Freedom of creative work was something dreamed about by the finest scientists of prerevolutionary Russia. Their thoughts and aspirations were movingly expressed in a letter which Konstantin Tsiolokovsky, a great Russian scientists, addressed to the Central Committee of the CPSU a few days before his death. "Only October," he wrote, "brought recognition to the works of a self-taught man. I came to feel the love of the people, and this gave me the strength to continue my work when I was already ill. However, illness now prevents me from completing the work I started.

"I hand over all that I have done on aviation, rocketry and interplanetary flights to the Party of Bolsheviks and to Soviet power, the real leaders of the progress of human culture. I am confident that they will successfully complete this work."

Only 25 years later the spaceship *Vostok,* piloted by the Soviet pilot-cosmonaut Yuri Gagarin, made the world's first orbital space flight. April 12, 1961 went down in history as the beginning of the space age.

The important constitutional guarantee of freedom to do creative work is the broad encouragement of invention and innovation. The development of mass scientific and technical creativity is a distinguishing feature of the Soviet way of life. The Soviet Government decree "On Inventions" (June 1919) laid down the foundations of the policy of the Soviet state in the sphere of invention. It read that, henceforth, all inventions belonged to the state and that they were to be placed at the disposal of all citizens and institutions. Soviet legislation ensured protection of inventors' rights for the first time in history and provided for the obligatory payment of fees for inventions. A special committee for the affairs of inventions was set up to guide technical creative work.

The first legislative acts of the Soviet state on invention were welcomed and supported by the working people. In 1922, three times more applications for the registration of inventions were submitted than in 1919.

Having set the course for the industrialization of the country, the Communist Party headed the movement for the rationalization of production. A particularly important role in promoting technical creative work, invention and innovation was played by the Central Committee's resolution "On the Status of Mass Invention from the Point of View of Rationalization of Production" (1930). In 1932, an All-Union Society of Inventors was set up, whose membership soon reached half a million. As years went by, this movement continued to grow so that it became necessary, for the overall guidance of technical creative work, to establish a special Committee for the Affairs of Inventions and Discoveries under the Council of People's Commissars. Between 1940 and 1979, the number of rationalization proposals and applications for the registration of inventions rose from 591,000 to more than 5 million.

At present the All-Union Society of Inventors and Innovators has a membership of more than 11 million. In addition there are 23 scientific and technical societies in the USSR, uniting 9.3 million engineers, technicians, specialists in agriculture, workers, farmers and students. In keeping with the USSR Constitution, the state provides the necessary material conditions for the development of mass technical creative work, renders support to voluntary societies, organizes the introduction of inventions and innovations in the national economy and other spheres of life, and protects the rights of inventors and innovators.

The Constitution of the USSR guarantees freedom of artistic creative-work. The Communist Party's policy in the sphere of literature and the arts is based on principles formulated by Lenin. There are no, nor can there be, he said, neutral artists siding with none of the forces taking part in social life and political struggle. Neutrality is also a stand, which objectively serves the interests of definite classes, social strata and groups. Therefore the Party invariably supports literature and arts that are openly linked with the revolutionary forces of the day.

Calling on artists to show independence of mind, Lenin vigorously opposed all attempts at a vulgar interpretation of the idea of partisanship, and came out against disregarding the complexity and specific features of creative work in the arts. He stressed that literature is least of all subject to mechanical adjustment or leveling, that in this field greater scope must be given to personal initiative, individual inclination, thought and fantasy, and that a search must be made in the sphere of form and content. "Art belongs to the people," he said. "Its roots should be deeply implanted in the very thick of the laboring masses. It should be understood and loved by the masses. It must unite and elevate their feelings, thoughts and will. It must stir to activity and develop the art instincts within them."[1]

In the first years of Soviet power the Party helped to establish and consolidate workers' organizations in the spheres of literature and the arts. In those years the biggest and the most democratic of them, and one that identified itself most closely with the tasks of the revolution, was the Proletkult (the proletari-

[1]V.I. Lenin, *On Literature and Art,* Progress Publishers, Moscow,1970, p. 251.

an cultural enlightenment organization), which concerned itself with all genres of artistic activity and which united a large army of professional and semiprofessional writers, who were primarily of working-class background.

However, the leaders of the Proletkult adopted positions which the Party could not support. They maintained that the working class must create its own, proletarian culture detached from the culture of the past, and that it was precisely they who were to provide leadership in the sphere of artistic creative work. (According to them, the Party was to guide the political struggle of the workers, the trade unions, their economic struggle, and the Proletkult, the "revolutionary-cultural-creative" struggle.) On December 1, 1920, the CPSU Central Committee published a resolution "On Proletkults." Resolutely condemning the positions of the leaders of the Proletkult, the Central Committee at the same time cautioned against tutelage of and putting pressure on writers and artists. "The Central Committee," the resolution read, "not only does not want to cripple the initiative of the workers' intelligentsia in the sphere of artistic, creative work but, on the contrary, wants to create a more healthy, normal atmosphere for it and to enable it to have a fruitful effect on all artistic work."

In another important resolution—"On the Policy of the Party in the Sphere of Imaginative Literature" (1925)—the Central Committee, stressed that "the Party as a whole can by no means commit to upholding any single trend *in the domain of literary form.*"

That is the position today too. Soviet writers and artists are completely free in their choice of subject matter and artistic form, and there exists the material basis for their exercise of the right to creative work, their right to choose the form in which to express their ideas and thoughts.

Replying to the accusations in the West that Soviet writers write "as bidden by the Party", Mikhail Sholokhov said: "That is not quite correct: Each of us writes as bidden by his heart, and our hearts belong to the Party and to our own people, whom we serve with our art."

In the Central Committee's report to the 26th Party Congress,

Leonid Brezhnev said: "To live with the interests of the people, to share their joys and grief, to assert the truth of life and our humanist ideas . . . this is precisely what spells out the genuine national character and the genuine Party commitment in art. True to the Leninist policy in culture, the Party takes a solicitous and respectful attitude to the artistic intelligentsia and orients it to the fulfillment of lofty, creative tasks."

An important social role is played by the unions of creative workers. The Union of Journalists has 68,000 members; the Union of Architects, nearly 16,000; the Union of Writers, about 9,000; the Union of Film Workers, almost 6,000; and the Union of Composers, more than 2,000. More than 50,000 people are united in the theatrical societies of the republics.

The unions and societies of creative workers are active in the publishing field. The Union of Writers of the USSR publishes 105 newspapers and magazines with a total daily circulation of 13.4 million copies. In 1980 the Soviet Writer Publishing House put out 463 books with a total printing of 21 million copies. Care for the work of writers, composers and artists is reflected in the Constitution's provision that the state creates the necessary material conditions for the development of literature and the arts, supports the unions of workers in the arts and protects the rights of authors.

More and more educational establishments training cultural workers are being built. Between 1960 and 1980 the number of musical, art and choreographic schools under the USSR Ministry of Culture rose from 1,750 to 7,700 (a 4.4-fold increase) and the number of their students reached 1.3 million. Three thousand specialists graduated from higher and specialized secondary schools in art and cinematography in 1940 and about 36,000 in 1980.

In keeping with the Constitution, not only professional art, but also amateur and folk arts are promoted in every way. The revolution made possible the participation of the broad masses in amateur art activities. In the very first years of Soviet power People's Commissar for Education Anatoly Lunacharsky noted "the tremendous instinctive enthusiasm of the masses for the arts and especially the theater. Thousands, if not tens of thousands of workers' and peasants' theatrical clubs have blossomed all over Russia. Thousands of young people flocked to all kinds of studios and schools, which proliferated in vast numbers."

Having originated as a mass, nonprofessional democratic movement uniting people of different trades and professions, nationalities, educational levels, social status and cultural backgrounds, amateur art activity has developed over the decades into diverse forms of popular art and has acquired a truly mass character. The country now has 1.1 million amateur art circles and groups—amateur theaters, philharmonic societies, pictorial and plastic arts and film studios, song and dance ensembles and choirs and orchestras which are attached to clubhouses, houses and palaces of culture and enterprises and educational establishments. More than 27 million people take part in them. Their activities are directed by people's art centers, methodological centers and amateur art centers run by the trade unions.

District, city, regional and republican amateur art reviews are held regularly. In 1976–77, the first All-Union Amateur Art Festival took place. It was devoted to the 60th anniversary of Soviet power. The All-Union Review of Amateur Films and the All-Union Exhibition of Amateur Artists and Applied Arts Masters have become major events in the cultural life of the country.

Traditional handicrafts are part of our culture. Our lacquered miniature paintings, paintings on wood, lace, chased metalwork, our carpets and amber decorations are internationally known. More than 200 traditional handicrafts are actively pursued by tens of thousands of masters in the USSR.

In a society of developed socialism, amateur art, like professional art, plays an important role in forming the artistic culture of a communist society.

CONCLUSION

1981 marks the 64th year of the Great October Socialist Revolution. Very great changes have taken place in the world in these years. Monarchies have fallen, fascist dictatorships have been swept away, imperialism's colonial system has collapsed. There has come into being a world socialist system which is constantly gaining strength. More and more countries and peoples embark on a socialist-oriented road. Imperialism is losing one position after another. One of the main reasons for the victorious march of socialism is that it provides an example of a more just organization of society, ensures genuine human rights and creates the most favorable conditions for the development of the individual, that it is a society of equal opportunities for all working people.

The experience of the USSR shows that socialism and human rights are inseparable. Just as socialism is unthinkable without human rights and freedoms, the genuine rights and freedoms of man are unthinkable without socialism.

As for the campaign around the alleged violation of human rights in the Soviet Union and other socialist countries, its organizers have grossly miscalculated. They are stepping on ice which is proving too thin. Their hypocrisy has been exposed by the book on human rights in the USA produced by the Communist Party of the United States. In the book the U.S. Communists draw the conclusion: "This capitalism—this system born of the slave trade and centuries of slavery, of child labor and the abuse of women, of contempt for those who labor and produce, with its adornments of male supremacy and elitism and racism and its products of colonialism and robber wars—this capitalism, through its politicians and penman, dares to lecture the world of socialism about morality and human rights!"[1]

For the overwhelming majority of the people in the capitalist countries the "freedoms and justice for all" proclaimed in bourgeois society are only a dream. "What, indeed," Leonid Brezhnev said, "can the apologists of the capitalist system oppose . . . real achievements of developed socialism? What real rights and freedoms are guaranteed to the masses in present-day imperialist society?

"The 'right' of tens of millions to unemployment? Or the 'right' of sick people to do without medical aid, the cost of which is enormous? Or the 'right' of ethnic minorities to humiliating discrimination in employment and education, in political and everyday life? Or is it the 'right' to live in perpetual fear of the omnipotent underworld or organized crime and to see how the press, cinema, TV and radio services are going out of their way to educate the younger generation in a spirit of selfishness, cruelty and violence?"

Such is the real state of things.

The reader may ask on what basis the "defenders of human rights" make their attacks on socialism. What they don't like is the provision of the USSR Constitution which says: "Enjoyment by citizens of their rights and freedoms must not be to the detriment of the interests of society and the state, or infringe upon the rights of other citizens." They regard the organic unity of citizens' rights and duties as an "intolerable limitation" of the rights of the individual, which is incompatible with democracy.

But the interconnection of citizens' rights and duties is a generally recognized principle of the democratic organization of social life. It is stated in the Universal Declaration of Human Rights adopted by the United Nations in 1948:

---

[1]*The State of Human Rights, USA*, New York, 1977, p. 43.

"1. Everyone has duties to the community in which alone the free and full development of his personality is possible.

"2. In the exercise of his rights and freedoms, everyone shall be subject only to such limitations as are determined by law solely for the purpose of securing due recognition and respect for the rights and freedoms of others and of meeting the just requirements of morality, public order and the general welfare in a democratic society."

This provision is written into the international covenants on human rights which are ratified and strictly observed by our country. The Soviet Constitution affirms this principle in the interests of our entire society and of every citizen.

It must be noted in this connection that the international covenants on human rights, which have been ratified by all the countries of the socialist community, are to this day not recognized by those who are the most vociferous about human rights. A U.S. political scientist, J. Green, wrote back in 1956 that "the United States would find it difficult to accept a treaty containing economic, social and cultural rights, because these went far beyond the rights contained in the United States Constitution."[1]

Soviet people, whose will is expressed in our Fundamental Law, hold that socialist democracy means the unity of rights and duties, of genuine freedom and civic responsibility and a harmonious combination of the interests of the society, the collective, and the individual. In the words of Lenin, it is "a discipline of comradeship, a discipline of the utmost mutual respect, a discipline of independence and initiative in the struggle."[2]

Socialist democracy is being constantly perfected. Implementation of the programs for socioeconomic and cultural development enables the socialist system to consistently extend the guarantees of citizens' rights and freedoms and improve the life of the people. The Party of Lenin is the principal guarantor of this advance.

"We have not yet attained communism," Leonid Brezhnev

---

[1] J. Green, *The United Nations and Human Rights,* Washington, 1956, p. 40.
[2] V.I. Lenin, *Collected Works,* Vol. 27, p. 515.

said. "But the whole world sees that our Party's activity and its aspirations are aimed to do everything necessary for the welfare of man, for the sake of man. It is this supreme and humane goal of the Party that gives it kinship with the people and creates firm and indissoluble bonds between it and all Soviet people."